DATA TRASH
the theory of the virtual class

CultureTexts

Arthur and Marilouise Kroker　　　　*General Editors*

Culture texts is a series of creative explorations in theory, politics and culture at the *fin de millennium*. Thematically focussed around key theoretical debates in the postmodern condition, the *CultureTexts* series challenges received discourses in art, social and political theory, feminism, science and technology and the body. Taken individually, contributions to *CultureTexts* represent the forward breaking-edge of postmodern theory and practice.

Titles

Spasm: Virtual Reality, Android Music and Electric Flesh
Arthur Kroker

The Last Sex: Feminism and Outlaw Bodies
edited and introduced by Arthur and Marilouise Kroker

Death at the Parasite Café
Stephen Pfohl

The Possessed Individual
Arthur Kroker

Ideology and Power in the Age of Lenin in Ruins
edited and introduced by Arthur and Marilouise Kroker

Seduction
Jean Baudrillard

The Hysterical Male: New Feminist Theory
edited and introduced by Arthur and Marilouise Kroker

Panic Encyclopedia
Arthur Kroker, Marilouise Kroker and David Cook

Life After Postmodernism: Essays on Value and Culture
edited and introduced by John Fekete

Body Invaders
edited and introduced by Arthur and Marilouise Kroker

The Postmodern Scene: Excremental Culture and Hyper-Aesthetics
Arthur Kroker/David Cook

DATA TRASH
the theory of the virtual class

Arthur Kroker
Michael A. Weinstein

New World Perspectives
Montreal

New World Perspectives
3652 Avenue Laval
Montreal, Canada
H2X 3C9
Fax: (514) 987-9724

ISBN 0-920393-23-3
Published simultaneously in the U.S.A. by St. Martin's Press.

Arthur Kroker's contribution to *Data Trash* was facilitated by a research grant
from the *Social Sciences and Humanities Research Council of Canada.*

Canadian Cataloguing in Publication Data

Kroker, Arthur , 1945-
    Data Trash :   the theory of the virtual class

(CultureTexts series)
Includes bibliographical references.
ISBN 0-920393-23-3

    1. United States—Civilization—1970-
2. Virtual Reality—United States.
3. Civilization, Modern—1950-   4. Computers and
civilization.   I. Weinstein, Michael A.
II. Title.   III.   Series.

E169.12.K77 1994   973.92   C94-900523-1

Printed and bound in Canada

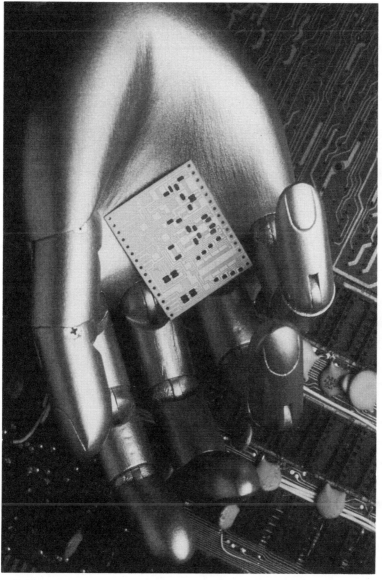

G. Gay
La Banque d'images

Stelarc
Photo: Tony Figallo

CONTENTS

PREFACE

DATA TRASH

Virtual Reality is the dream of pure telematic experience. Beginning in the cybernetic shadowland of head-mounted scanners, wired gloves, and data suits, virtual reality has quickly become the electronic horizon of the twenty-first century. A cold world where bodies get prepped for downloading into data, where seeing means artificial optics, where hearing is listening to the high-speed world of sampler culture, where travelling becomes a nomadic journey across the MUD (*Multiple User Dungeons*), and where communication disappears into the high-speed fibre "backbone" of the Internet. In virtual reality, flesh vaporizes into virtuality as (twentieth-) century bodies are repackaged with (twenty-first-) century cybernetic nervous systems for speeding across the electronic frontier.

The gigantic nova of technotopia pulses with such brilliant energy because western society is in the terminal phase of a slow, but nonetheless fatal, fade-out. A prolonged evacuation of the energies of the social where the biological organism flips into the electronic body, and where the cult of the "wired" is the ruling rhetoric of all the technological fetishists.

The wired body is perfect. Travelling like an electronic nomad through the circulatory flows of the mediascape, it possesses only the virtual biological form of a multi-layered scanner image. Abandoning the heavy referential history of a central nervous system, the wired body actually *grows* a telematic nervous system that is freely distributed across the electronic mirror of the Internet. A product of neural tapping and image-processing, the wired body is the (technoid) life-form that finally cracks its way out of the dead shell of human culture.

Technotopia is about disappearances: the vanishing of the body (into a relational data base), the nervous system into "distributive processing," and the skin into wetware. As technology comes alive as a distinctive species, we finally encounter the end of (human) history and the beginning of virtual history. A waiting time of *growing bodies* for endless circulation through all the synapses and gateways of the data networks. A euphoric space where subjectivity drains away into televisual memories, and desire is recombined into a vertiginous matrix of doubled possibilities. Virtual reality skin-grafts the logic of the ambivalent sign onto the "standing reserve" of the social. Here the delirium of the recline of western civilization is experienced as both the ecstasy of crash culture and the catastrophe of *our* burn-out in digital culture.

Cyber-Flesh
Scanning the Media-Net

Taking virtual reality as the (ir)real world of the electronic frontier, *Data Trash* operates like a deep space galactic explorer. Approaching the media-net with long-distance (theory) scans, it sweeps the virtual world with a rapid series of media probes, mapping the political economy of virtual reality and recombinant culture. It then arcs away with some final sampler images of crash history. Here, technology means the will to virtuality, and virtuality is about the recline of western civilization, an historical non-time marked by recurrent bouts of spasmodic violence and random crashes of all the big referents, which are all horizoned by the ascendant politics of liberal- and retro-fascism. Unlike the 1890s with its romantic invocation of catastrophe scenarios, the 1990s emerge as an era of general cultural recline: a time of cynical romanticism and cold love, where the body disappears into a virtual imaging-system, and where even catastrophes are reversed by the media-net into specular publicity for a crash that will never happen. On the one hand, the weakened body becomes a prosthetic to the media-net; and on the other the body electronic is data trash struggling to come alive again in recombinant form: to quick-learn how to survive the spasms and crashes of (digital) life on the virtual road. Reclining (into virtuality) *and* data trash (with a will?) This is the fate of the body electronic in the interminable countdown to the Year 2000.

Focussing on contemporary American politics but developing a more general historical thesis, *Data Trash* traces the will to virtuality as it becomes the primal impulse of pan-capitalism (virtual political economy), the mediascape (virtual culture), and post-history (virtual history). Using the literary device of media event-scenes, the theoretical analysis of *Data Trash* is mutated and accelerated by ongoing transformations in the cultural politics of the media-net. And why not? *Data Trash* is itself a wavering event-scene: a violent interzone between the will to virtuality and battered (human) flesh.

CHAPTER ONE

The Theory of the Virtual Class

Wired Shut

Wired intends to profit from the Internet. And so do a lot of others. "People are going to have to realize that the Net is another medium, and it has to be sponsored commercially and it has to play by the rules of the marketplace," says John Battelle, *Wired's* 28-year old managing editor. "You're still going to have sponsorship, advertising, the rules of the game, because it's just necessary to make commerce work." "I think that a lot of what some of the original Net god-utopians were thinking," continued Battelle, "is that there was just going to be this sort of huge anarchist, utopian, bliss medium, where there are no rules and everything is just sort of open. That's a great thought, but it's not going to work. And when the Time Warners get on the Net in a hard fashion it's going to be the people who first create the commerce and the environment, like *Wired*, that will be the market leaders."

Andrew Leonard, "Hot-Wired"
The Bay Guardian

The twentieth-century ends with the growth of cyber-authoritarianism, a stridently pro-technotopia movement, particularly in the mass media, typified by an obsession to the point of hysteria with emergent technologies, and with a consistent and very deliberate attempt to shut down, silence, and exclude any perspectives critical of technotopia. Not a wired culture, but a virtual culture that is wired shut: compulsively fixated on digital technology as a source of salvation from the reality of a lonely culture and radical social disconnection from everyday life, and determined to exclude from public debate any perspective that is not a cheerleader for the coming-to-be of the fully realized technological society. The virtual class is populated by would-be astronauts who never got the chance to go to the moon, and they do not easily accept criticism of this new Apollo project for the body telematic.

This is unfortunate since it is less a matter of being pro- or anti-technology, but of developing a critical perspective on the ethics of virtuality. When technology mutates into virtuality, the direction of political debate becomes clarified. If we cannot escape the hard-wiring of (our) bodies into wireless culture, then how can we inscribe primary ethical concerns onto the will to virtuality? How can we turn the virtual horizon in the direction of substantive human values: aesthetic creativity, social solidarity, democratic discourse, and economic justice? To link the relentless drive to cyberspace with ethical concerns is, of course, to give the lie to technological liberalism. To insist, that is, that the coming-to-be of the will to virtuality, and with it the emergence of our doubled fate as either body dumps or hyper-texted bodies, virtualizers or data trash, does not relax the traditional human injunction to give primacy to the ethical ends of the technological purposes we choose (or the will to virtuality that chooses us).

Privileging the question of ethics via virtuality lays bare the impulse to nihilism that is central to the virtual class. For it, the drive to planetary mastery represented by the will to virtuality relegates the ethical suasion to the electronic trashbin. Claiming with monumental hubris to be already beyond good and evil, it assumes perfect equivalency between the will to virtuality and the will to the (virtual) good. If the good is equivalent to the disintegration of experience into cybernetic interactivity or to the disappearance of memory and solitary reflection into massive Sunstations of archived information, then the virtual class is the leading exponent of the era of telematic ethics. Far from having abandoned ethical concerns, the virtual class has patched a coherent, dynamic, and comprehensive system of ethics onto the hard-line processors of the will to virtuality. Against economic justice, the virtual class practices a mixture of predatory capitalism and gung-ho technocratic rationalizations for laying waste to social concerns for employment, with insistent demands for "restructuring economies," "public policies of labor adjustment," and "deficit cutting," all aimed at maximal profitability. Against democratic discourse, the virtual class institutes anew the authoritarian mind, projecting its class interests onto cyberspace from which vantage-point it crushes any and all dissent to the prevailing orthodoxies of technotopia. For the virtual class, politics is about absolute control over intellectual property by means of war-like strategies of communication, control, and command. Against social solidarity, the virtual class promotes a grisly form of raw social materialism, whereby social experience is reduced to its prosethetic after-effects: the body becomes a passive archive to be processed, entertained, and stockpiled by the seduction-apertures of the virtual reality complex. And finally, against aesthetic creativity, the virtual class promotes the value of pattern-maintenance (of its own choosing), whereby human intelligence is reduced to a circulating medium of cybernetic exchange floating in the interfaces of the cultural animation machines. Key to the success of the virtual class is its promotion of a radically diminished vision of human experience and of a disintegrated conception of the human good: for virtualizers, the good is ultimately that which disappears human subjectivity, substituting the war-machine of cyberspace for the data trash of experience. Beyond this, the virtual class can achieve dominance today because its reduced vision of human experience consists of a digital superhighway, a fatal scene of circulation and gridlock, which corresponds to how the late twentieth-century mind likes to see itself. *Reverse nihilism*: not the nihilistic will as projected outwards onto an external object, but the nihilistic will turned inwards, decomposing subjectivity, reducing the self to an object of conscience- and body vivisectioning. What does it mean when the body is virtualized without a sustaining ethical vision? Can anyone be strong enough for this? What results is rage against the body: a hatred of existence that can only be satisfied by an abandonment of flesh and subjectivity and, with it, a flight into virtuality. Virtuality without ethics is a primal scene of social suicide: a site of mass cyrogenics where bodies are quick-frozen for future resequencing by the archived data networks. The virtual class can be this dynamic because it is already the after-shock of the living dead: body vivisectionists and early (mind) abandoners surfing the Net on a road trip to the virtual Inferno.

"Adapt or You're Toast"

The virtual class has driven to global power along the digital superhighway. Representing perfectly the expansionary interests of the recombinant commodity-form, the virtual class has seized the imagination of contemporary culture by conceiving a techno-utopian high-speed cybernetic grid for travelling across the electronic frontier. In this mythology of the new technological frontier, contemporary society is either equipped for fast travel down the main arterial lanes of the information highway, or it simply ceases to exist as a functioning member of technotopia. As the CEO's and the specialist consultants of the virtual class triumphantly proclaim: "Adapt or you're toast."

We now live in the age of dead information, dead (electronic) space, and dead (cybernetic) rhetoric. *Dead information?* That's our cooptation as servomechanisms of the cybernetic grid (the digital superhighway) that swallows bodies, and even whole societies, into the dynamic momentum of its telematic logic. Always working on the basis of the illusion of enhanced interactivity, the digital superhighway is really about the full immersion of the flesh into its virtual double. As *dead (electronic) space*, the digital superhighway is a big real estate venture in cybernetic form, where competing claims to intellectual property rights in an array of multi-media technologies of communication are at stake. No longer capitalism under the doubled sign of consumer and production models, the digital superhighway represents the disappearance of capitalism into colonized virtual space. And *dead (cybernetic) rhetoric?* That's the Internet's subordination to the predatory business interests of a virtual class, which might pay virtual lip service to the growth of electronic communities on a global basis, but which is devoted in actuality to shutting down the anarchy of the Net in favor of virtualized (commercial) exchange. Like a mirror image, the digital superhighway always means its opposite: not an open telematic autoroute for fast circulation across the electronic galaxy, but an immensely seductive harvesting machine for delivering bodies, culture, and labor to virtualization. The information highway is paved with (our) flesh. So consequently, *the theory of the virtual class*: cultural accomodation to technotopia is its goal, political consolidation (around the aims of the virtual class) its method, multi-media nervous systems its relay, and (our) disappearance into pure virtualities its ecstatic destiny.

That there is an inherent political contradiction between the attempt by the virtual class to liquidate the sprawling web of the Internet in favor of the smooth telematic vision of the digital superhighway is apparent. The information highway is the antithesis of the Net, in much the same way as the virtual class must destroy the *public dimension* of the Internet for its own survival. The informational technology of the Internet as a new *force* of virtual production provides the social conditions necessary for instituting fundamentally new *relations* of electronic creation. Spontaneously and certainly against the long-range interests of the virtual class, the Internet has been swamped by demands for meaning. Newly screen-radiated scholars dream up visions of a Virtual University, the population of Amsterdam goes on-line as Digital City, environmentalists become web weavers as they form a global Green cybernetic informational grid, and a new generation of fiction writers develops forms of telematic writing that mirror the crystalline structures and multi-phasal connections of hypertext.

But, of course, for the virtual class, content slows the speed of virtualized exchange, and meaning becomes the antagonistic contradiction of data. Accordingly, demands for meaning must be immediately denied as just another road-kill along the virtual highway. As such, the virtual class exercises its intense obsessive-compulsive drive to subordinate society to the telematic mythology of the digital superhighway. The democratic possibilities of the Internet, with its immanent appeal to new forms of global communication, might have been the seduction-strategy appropriate for the construction of the digital superhighway, but now that the cybernetic grid is firmly in control, the virtual class must move to liquidate the Internet. It is an old scenario, repeated this time in virtual form. Marx understood this first: every technology releases opposing possibilities towards emancipation and domination. Like its early bourgeois predecessors at the birth of capitalism, the virtual class christens the birth of technotopia by suppressing the potentially emancipatory relations of production released by the Internet in favor of the traditionally predatory force of production signified by the digital superhighway. Data is the anti-virus of meaning—telematic information refuses to be slowed down by the drag-weight of content. And the virtual class seeks to exterminate the *social* possibilities of the Internet. These are the first lessons of the theory of the virtual class.

Information Highway/Media-Net: Virtual Pastoral Power

The "information highway" has become the key route into virtuality. The "information highway" is another term for what we call the "media-net." It's a question of whether we're cruising on a highway or being caught up in a Net, always already available for (further) processing. The "highway" is definitely an answer to "Star Wars": the communications complex takes over from the "military-industrial complex." Unlike "Star Wars," however, the "highway" has already (de-)materialized in the world behind the monitors: cyber-space. For crash theory there is an irony:the highway is a trompe l'oeil of possessive individualism covering the individual possessed by the net, sucked into the imploded, impossible world behind the screen—related to the dubious world of ordinary perception through cyber-space.

Information Highway vs. Media-Net

The prophet-hypesters of the information highway, from President Bill Clinton, U.S.A., to President Bill Gates, Microsoft, proclaim a revolution to a higher level of bourgeois consciousness. The highway is the utopia of the possessive individual: the possessive individual now resides in technotopia.

This is how the higher level of bourgeois consciousness comes to be in grades of perfection. Firstly, we enter an information highway which promises the "individual" access to "information" from the universal archive instantly and about anything. The capacity of the Net to hold information is virtually infinite and, with the inevitable advances in microprocessors, its capacities to gather, combine, and relay information will be equal to any demand for access. Are you curious about anything? The answer is right at your fingertips. More seriously, do you need to know something? A touch of a button will get you what you need and eventually your brain waves alone (telekinesis fantasy) will do it. Here is the world as information completely at the beck and call of the possessive individual (the individual, that is, who is *possessed* by information). Here, everyone is a god who, if they are not omniscient all at once, can at least entertain whatever information that they wish to have at any time they wish to have it. Information is not the kind of thing that has to be shared. If everyone all at once wanted to know who won the Stanley Cup in 1968 they could have the information simultaneously: cyber-space as the site of Unamuno's panarchy, where each one is king.

At the next grade of perfection, the highway not only provides access to that which is already given, but allows the "individual" to "interact" with other "individuals," to create a society in cyber-space. The freedom to access information will be matched by the freedom to access individuals anywhere and at any time, since eventually everyone will be wired. The hybridization of television, telephone, and computer will produce every possible refinement of mediated presence, allowing interactors an unprecedented range of options for finely adjusting the distance of their relations. Through the use of profiles, data banks, and bulletin boards people will be able to connect with exactly those who will give them the most satisfaction, with whom they share interests, opinions, projects, and sexual preferences, and for whom they have need. Just as "individuals" will be able to access the realm of "information" (anything from their financial and insurance records to any movie ever made), they will also be able to access the domain of "human" communicators to find the ones who are best suited to them. As Bill Gates of Microsoft puts it: "The opportunity for people to reach out and share is amazing."[1]

The information highway as technotopia is the place where "individuals" command information for whatever purposes they entertain and find others with whom to combine to pursue those purposes. As Gates puts it, it is "empowering stuff." Technotopia is the seduction by which the flesh is drawn into the Net. What seduces is the fantasy of "empowerment," the center of the contemporary possessive individualist complex. By having whatever information one wants instantly and without effort, and by being linked to appropriate associates one saves an immense amount of time and energy, and is more likely to make better decisions for oneself. Who can complain about having more information, especially if it can be accessed easily and appropriately by a system of selectors that gives you what you ask for and nothing else, or even better, that knows you so well that it gives you what you really want (need?) (is good for you?), but did not even realize that you wanted?

The information highway means the death of the (human) agent and the triumph of the expert program, the wisdom that the greatest specialist would give you. Expert programs to diagnose you. Medical tests performed at home while you are hooked up to a computer that are interpreted by an expert program. In order to serve you, the "highway" will demand information from you. The selector systems will have to get to know you, scan you, monitor you, give you periodic tests. The expert program will be the new center for pastoral power. This is, of course, still enacted under capitalism. You will have to pay for information with money and there will be plenty of restrictions on its accessibility. Leave that as a contradiction of the virtual class between the capitalist organization of the highway and its technotopian vision: a contradiction within possessive individualism. More importantly, you will pay for information with information; indeed, you will be information.

The highway becomes the Net. What appears as "empowerment" is a trompe l'oeil, a seduction, an entrapment in a Baudrillardian loop in which the Net elicits information from the "user" and gives it back in what the selectors say is an appropriate form for that user. The great agent of possibility becomes the master tool of normalization, now a micro-normalization with high specificity ... perhaps uniqueness! Each "individual" has a unique disciplinary solution to hold them fast to the Net, where they are dumped for image processing and image reception. The information highway is the way by which bodies are drawn into cyber-space through the seduction of empowerment.

Bourgeois masculinity has always been pre-pubescent: the thoughts of little boys thinking about what they would do if they controlled the world, but now the world is cyber-space. The dream of being the god of cyber-space—public ideology as the fantasy of pre-pubescent males: a regression from sex to an autistic power drive.

Against the Virtual Class

The virtual class holds on to its worldview with cynicism or with vicious naivete. It is a compound of late nineteenth-century Darwinian capitalism (retro-industrial Darwinism) and tech-hype. After what has happened so far in the twentieth-century and is still going on in the way of technological carnage, it is amusing to realize that there are still techno-fetishists filled with enthusiasm about how technology is going to fulfill their pre-pubescent dream, which they assume unthinkingly that everyone inevitably shares with them. Why? Is it so clear that technology cannot serve anything else than the last man as the pre-pubescent boy who would like nothing else but to play video games forever?

The retro-child. The virtual class is in its utopian visionary phase, filled with cyber-worlds to conquer. What will it be in its consolidation phase when we are fully entrapped in the Net and it starts tightening around us? Normalization will come here too. Radically empowering computer land is the utopia of a rising class identifying its peculiar occupational psychosis with (a wired) "humanity." When we are immersed in the Net the fiction of the "possessive individual" will be discarded from the virtual class's ideology in favor of some sort of defense of cyber-slavery, in which the virtual class affirms its own slavery, along with that of all the rest, to the Net. This will be the culminating moment of the ascetic priests (Nietzsche). One can only think of Jonestown. The virtual class ushers itself and everyone else into the Net to serve it as image/information resources and as image/information receptors. Wired into the command functions at work and wired into the sensibility functions when off work: the body as a function of cyber-space.

Panic Information Highway

Organizations are in a panic stampede to get on the "information highway," to be players in cyber-space. Everyone wants in on the exploitation of the new frontier and even more they don't want to be killed in the real world, which will be managed ever-increasingly from cyber-space; not to mention the efficiencies of the Net. For the moment the advantages of the Net are not that obvious once you get on, but that is only a temporary situation. The Net is filling up fast with everything imaginable and it's indefinitely expandable.

There is another kind of panic in process about the "information highway." This one from the concerned liberals who are afraid of the power of those who will determine the configuration of the highway. In his report on Bill Gates, John Seabrook provides an enlightening glimpse of Gates's character along with cautionary warnings. We are concerned with the latter, with a specimen of the liberal ideology which counts as the major ideological resistance to cyber tech-hype.

Seabrook frames his warnings within a bit of short-range futurology. There is a new kind of computer on the way that will change our lives in incalculable ways: "The new machine will be a communications device that connects people to the information highway. It will penetrate far beyond the fifteen per cent of American households that now own a computer, and it will control, or absorb, other communications machines now in people's homes—the phone, the fax, the television. It will sit in the living room, not in the study."[2] The cyber command-machine: the entrance to the highway: the lip of the Net.

Seabrook notes that Bill Gates's current ambition is to have Microsoft be the source of "the standard operating-system software for the information-highway machine, just as it now supplies the standard operating-system software, called Windows, for the personal computer."[3] The standard operating-system will be the program that makes possible specific uses of the Net, all across the Net. Seabrook believes that by supplying the standard operating-system software for the "information-highway machine" Gates would gain great power: "If Gates does succeed in providing the operating system for the new machine, he will have tremendous influence over the way people communicate with one another: he, more than anyone else, will determine what it is like to use the information highway."[4]

Seabrook shows a misunderstanding here of the "influence" of the virtual class. What is the "influence" of a standard operating-system? Would there be major differences among possible alternative competing operating-systems for the information-highway machine that would alter significantly "the way people communicate with each other?" Or, as with the phone system, is the object simply to facilitate entry into the Net? If the latter is so, no power in any conventional sense accrues to the organizational leader who wins the competition to supply the system. Gates understands this. He wrote to Seabrook that "the digital revolution is all about facilitation-creating tools to make things easy."[5] This is the gospel of the last man, not of the "technology-oriented dictator" that one of his competitors is afraid that Gates might become. There is greater power, of a wholly different kind than the conventional power to order people around, in ushering people into the Net, in being the agent of technological dependency. This is the power of silent seduction, of giving accessibility to cyber-space. Bill Gates is not Zeus, casting thunderbolts, but Charon, taking us across the electronic Styx into virtuality. Seabrook, the techno-humanist liberal on a diversionary mission, is concerned with what goes into cyber-space. He accepts the techno-hype and is afraid of a techno-fascism that he refuses to acknowledge has already been instituted. Gates only cares that we all get into cyber-space: the seducer as great facilitator.

Gates, indeed, has no interest in the conventional politics of the communication revolution. As much as Seabrook tried to get him to acknowledge the question of power, Gates would resist. He made his position plain in commenting that the highway would have some "secondary effects that people will worry about." That is not his problem, however: "We are involved in creating a new media but it is not up to us to be the censors or referees of this media—it is up to public policy to make those decisions."[6]

"Public policy" is what goes on to get the flesh to adjust to the Net. The greater project is beyond policy, transcendent to it—that is the project of wiring bodies to the Net. That everyone will be wired to the information-highway machine is an historical inevitability that puts politics in its place as a local clean-up activity around the Net. This is technotopianism in its purest and most cynical form. Compare it to that other computer entrepreneur, the retro-fascist Ross Perot, who uses the wealth he has gained from the information industry to finance his appeal to a nationalistic policy. The technotopian has no such leanings, but with vicious naivete depends on liberal-fascist allies in government to protect the Net. Gates has identified himself with Technology, the greater power, the one that will finally be decisive. Through the silent seduction of the operating-system.

The Virtual Class and Capitalism

The computer industry is in an intensive phase of "creative destruction," the term coined by Schumpeter and used by the neo- Darwinian macho apologists for capitalism to refer to the economic killing fields produced by rapid technological change. The Net is being brought into actuality through the offices of ruthless capitalist competition, in which vast empires fall and rise within a single decade (Big Blue/Microsoft). Under the disciplinary liberal night watchman's protection of "private" property-rights, capitalist freebooters destroy one another as they race to be the ones who actualize the Net, just like the railroads of the nineteenth-century racing across the continent. This means that the virtual class retains a strict capitalist determination and that its representative social type must be a capitalist, someone who is installing the highway to win a financial competition, if nothing else. If one is not so minded in today's computer industry they will be eaten alive. You will only be able to get personal kicks and pursue your (ressentiment-laden) idealistic views of computer democracy in this industry if you sell. So you hype your ideas and your ideals become hype—that is the twisted psychology of the virtual class: not hyped ideology, but something of, by, and for the Net: ideological hype.

There are pure capitalists in the cyber industry and there are capitalists who are also visionary computer specialists. The latter, in a spirit of vicious naivete, generate the ideological hype, a messianic element, that the former take up cynically. It's the old story of the good cop and the bad cop. How come the good cop tolerates the bad cop? So much for the computer democracy of cyber possessive-individualists. The economic base of the virtual class is the entire communications industry—everywhere it reaches. As a whole, this industry processes ideological hype for capitalist ends. It is most significantly constituted by cynicism, not viciously naive vision. Yet, though a small group in numerical proportion to the whole virtual class, the visionaries are essential to cyber-capitalism because they provide the ideological mediation to seduce the flesh into the Net. In this sense the cynical capitalists and the well-provided techies are merely drones, clearing the way for the Pied Piper's parade.

A frontier mentality rules the drive into cyber-space. It is one of the supreme ironies that a primitive form of capitalism, a retro-capitalism, is actualizing virtuality. The visionary cyber-capitalist is a hybrid monster of social Darwinism and techno-populist individualism. It is just such an imminently reversible figure that can provide the switching mechanism back and forth between cyber-space and the collapsing space of (crashed) perception.

The most complete representative of the virtual class is the visionary capitalist who is constituted by all of its contradictions and who, therefore, secretes its ideological hype. The rest of the class tends to split the contradictions: the visionless-cynical-business capitalists and the perhaps visionary, perhaps skill-oriented, perhaps indifferent techno-intelligentsia of cognitive scientists, engineers, computer scientists, video-game developers, and all the other communication specialists, ranged in hierarchies, but all dependent for their economic support on the drive to virtualization. Whatever contradictions there are within the virtual class—that is, the contradictions stemming from the confrontation of bourgeois and proletarian—the class as a whole supports the drive into cyber-space through the wired world. This is the way it works in post late-capitalism, where the communication complex is repeating the pattern of class collaborationism that marked the old military-industrial complex. The drive into the Net is one of those great capitalist techno-projects that depends upon a concert of interests to sustain it, as it sucks social energy into itself. The phenomenon of a collaborationist complex harboring a retro-Darwinian competition is something new, but is stabilized, in the final analysis, by a broad consensus among the capitalist components of the virtual class that the liberal-fascist state structure is deserving of support. Indeed, in the U.S.A. in the 1990s the state is the greatest producer of the ideological hype of the "information highway." The virtual class has its administration in the White House. The concerted drive into cyber-space proceeds, all in the name of economic development and a utopian imaginary of possessive individualists.

The Hyper-Texted Body or Nietzsche Gets a Modem

But why be nostalgic? The old body type was always OK, but the wired body with its micro-flesh, multi-media channeled ports, cybernetic fingers, and bubbling neuro-brain finely interfaced to the "standard operating-system" of the Internet is infinitely better. Not really the wired body of sci-fi with its mutant designer look, or body flesh with its ghostly reminders of nineteenth-century philosophy, but the hyper-texted body as both: a wired nervous system embedded in living (dedicated) flesh.

The hyper-texted body with its dedicated flesh? That is our telematic future, and it's not necessarily so bleak. Technology has always been our sheltering environment: not second-order nature, but primal nature for the twenty-first-century body. In the end, the virtual class is very old-fashioned. It clings to an antiquated historical form—capitalism—and, on its behalf, wants to shut down the creative possibilities of the Internet. Dedicated flesh rebels against the virtual class. It does not want to be interfaced to the Net through modems and external software black boxes, but *actually wants to be an Internet*. The virtual class wants to appropriate emergent technologies for purposes of authoritarian political control over cyberspace. It wants to drag technotopia back to the age of the primitive politics of predatory capitalism. But dedicated (geek) flesh wants something very different. Unlike the (typically European) rejection of technotopia in favor of a newly emergent nostalgia movement under the sign of "Back to Vinyl" in digital sound or "Back to Pencils" in literature, dedicated flesh wants to deeply instantiate the age of technotopia. Operating by means of the aesthetic strategy of over-identification with the feared and desired object, the hyper-texted body insists that ours is already the era of post-capitalism, and even post-technology. Taking the will to virtuality seriously, it demands its telematic rights to be a functioning interfaced body: to be a multi-media thinker, to patch BUS ports on its cyber-flesh as it navigates the gravity well of the Internet, to create aesthetic visions equal to the pure virtualities found everywhere on the now superceded digital superhighway, and to become data to such a point of violent implosion that the body finally breaks free of the confining myth of "wired culture" and goes wireless.

The wireless body? That is the floating body, drifting around in the debris of technotopia: encrypted flesh in a sea of data. The perfect evolutionary successor to twentieth-century flesh, the wireless body fuses the speed of virtualized exchange into its cellular structure. DNA-coated data is inserted directly through spinal taps into dedicated flesh for better navigation through the treacherous shoals of the electronic galaxy. Not a body without memory or feelings, but the opposite. The wireless body is the battleground of the major political and ethical conflicts of late-twentieth- and early-twenty-first-century experience.

Perhaps the wireless body will be just a blank data dump, a floating petrie-dish where all the brilliant residues of technotopia are mixed together in newly recombinant forms. In this case, the wireless body would be an indefinitely reprogrammable chip: micro-soft flesh where the "standard operating-system" of the new electronic age comes off the top of the TV set, flips inside the body organic, and is soft-wired to a waiting vat of remaindered flesh.

But the wireless body could be, and already is, something very different. Not the body as an organic grid for passively sampling all the drifting bytes of recombinant culture, but the wireless body as a highly-charged theoretical and political site: a moving field of aesthetic contestation for remapping the galactic empire of technotopia. Data flesh can speak so confidently of the possibility of multi-media democracy, of sex without secretions, and of integrated (cyber-) relationships because it has already burst through to the other side of technotopia: to that point of brilliant dissolution where the Net comes alive, and begins to speak the language of wireless bodies in a wireless world.

There are already many wireless bodies on the Internet: Many data travellers on the virtual road have managed under the weight of the predatory capitalism of the virtual class and the even weightier humanist prejudices against geek flesh, to make of the Internet a charmed site for fusing the particle waves of all the passing data into a new body type: hyper-texted bodies circulating as "web weavers" in electronic space.

Refusing to be remaindered as flesh dumped by the virtual class, the hyper-texted body bends virtuality to its own purposes. Here, the will to virtuality ceases to be one-dimensional, becoming a doubled process, grisly yet creative, spatial yet memoried, in full violent play as the hyper-texted body. Always schizoid yet fully integrated, the hyper-texted body swallows its modem, cuts its wired connections to the information highway, and becomes its own system-operating software, combining and remutating the surrounding data storm into new virtualities. And why not? Human flesh no longer exists, except as an incept of the wireless world. Refuse, then, nostalgia for the surpassed past of remaindered flesh, and hyper-text your way to the (World Wide) Webbed body: the body that actually dances on its own data organs, sees with multi-media graphical interface screens, makes new best tele-friends on the MOO, writes electronic poetry on the disappearing edges of video, sound, and text integrators, and insists on going beyond the tedious world of binary divisions to the new cyber-mathematics of FITS. The hyper-texted body, then, is the precursor of a new world of multi-media politics, fractalized economics, incept personalities, and (cybernetically) interfaced relationships. After all, why should the virtual class monopolize digital reality? It only wants to suppress the creative possibilities of virtualization, privileging instead the tendencies of technotopia towards new and more vicious forms of cyber-authoritarianism. The virtual class only wants to subordinate digital reality to the will to capitalism. The hyper-texted body responds to the challenge of virtualization by making itself a monstrous double: pure virtuality/pure flesh. Consequently, our telematic future: the wireless body on the Net as a sequenced chip micro-programmed by the virtual class for purposes of (its) maximal profitability, or the wireless body as the leading-edge of critical subjectivity in the twenty-first century. If the virtual class is the post-historical successor to the early bourgeoisie of primitive capitalism, then the hyper-texted body is the Internet equivalent of the Paris Commune: anarchistic, utopian, and in full revolt against the suppression of the general (tele-)human possibilities of the Net in favor of the specific (monetary) interests of the virtual class. Always already the past to the future of the hyper-texted body, the virtual class is the particular interest that must be overcome by the hyper-texted body of data trash if the Net is to be gatewayed by soft ethics.

Soft ethics? Nietzsche's got a modem, and he is already rewriting the last pages of *The Will to Power* as *The Will to Virtuality*. As the patron saint of the hyper-texted body, Nietzsche is data trash to the smooth, unbroken surface of the virtual class.

Soft Ideology

So then, some road maps for following the digital route taken by the virtual class across the landscape of the body recombinant.

Map 1: The Digital Superhighway as Ruling Metaphor

The high-speed digital superhighway is the ruling metaphor of the virtual class. As the class that specializes in virtualized exchange, the information superhighway allows the virtual class to speak in the language of encrypted data, circulate through all the capillaries of digital, fibre optic electric space, and float at hyper-speed to the point where data melts down into pure vitualities. The information superhighway is the playground of the virtual class. While defining the virtual class, it is also the privileged monopoly of global data communication.

As the language of the virtual class, the information superhighway is where the virtual class lives, dreams, works, and conspires. Not accessible to all, the information superhighway with its accelerated transfers of data, voice, and video is open only to those possessing the privileged corporate codes. And not evident to everyone, the information superhighway is also a site of global power because it remains an invisible, placeless, floating electronic space to the un-virtualized classes, to those, that is, who have been abandoned by the flight of the virtual class to the telematic future. Here, virtual power is about invisibility: the endocolonization of the unwired world of time, history, and human flesh by the electronic body.

A space-binding technological medium of communication, the information superhighway invests the electronic body of the virtual class with a new language, fit for twenty-first-century simu-flesh and fibrillated nerve tissue. Neither the late twentieth-century language of cyberspace (with its romantic invocation of pure electronic space as the site of a "consensual hallucination") nor the traditional laboratory language of recombinant genetics, the information superhighway speaks the digital language of the world's first post-flesh body. Post-flesh? That is the electronic body of the virtual class: accessed by serial arrays of BUS ports, animated by its 3-D graphic interfaces, coded in its Web by its designated URL's (Uniform Resource Locators), energized by the telematic dream of instantly disposable cybersex machines, and reduced in its bodily movements to a twitching finger (on the cyber-dial). The electronic body is equipped with a surfer's consciousness, and is obsessed with its own disappearance into the inertial gridlock of high-speed. A pure virtuality, the electronic body is always in flight (from itself): it constitutes a sampler spectrum of the media force-fields which it navigates with the assistance of communication satellites parked in deep-space orbital trajectories. Certainly not a cyber-body, a "pure virtuality" is where the electronic body is reborn as a living, (telematically) breathing simu-flesh: a specimen of evolutionary implosion where technology merges with biology, the result being the post-flesh body of the virtual class. Not a passively engineered product of recombinant genetics, the electronic body as a pure virtuality has its neural synapses coded with an instinctual drive to cut, clone, and retranscribe the genetic strips of new media culture. Multi-media by nature, space-binding by instinct, and driven by an obsession compulsion towards its own disappearance down the information superhighway, the electronic body of the virtual class is the first mutant-body type to appear on the long-range scanners of the awaiting twenty-first-century.

Map 2: The Information "Superhighway" Does Not Exist

Or maybe it is just the opposite? If the information superhighway can be the ruling sign of the virtual class it is because it has no existence other than that of an old modernist metaphor concealing the disappearance of technology into virtuality, information into data, and the highway into space-binding electronic circuitry. In this case, the concept of the information superhighway simultaneously performs a revealing and concealing function with respect to the virtual class. It reveals the deep association of this class with high-speed virtualized exchange, but it conceals the drive to global power on the part of the virtual class in favor of a comforting, romantic myth of outlaw travel across the electronic frontier.

Take apart the dense ideogram of the information superhighway to see what is inside and all the political tactics of the virtual class suddenly spill out: its promotional rhetoric, its policing methods, its doubled strategy of an ideology of facilitation and an actuality of virtualization, its ruling illusions of immersion and interactivity, and its missionary commitment to technotopia. The opposition to the virtual class also emerges: a growing political critique based on hyper-nostalgia ("Back to Vinyl"), reinforced by an alternative aesthetic refusal of the virtual class based on over-identification with the electronic body ("Data Trash").

Map 3: Seduce and Virtualize

Functioning as the political ideology of the virtual class, the information highway delivers up the body to virtualization. While its promotional rhetoric is cloaked in a seductive ideology of facilitation, in actuality the ruling metaphor of the information superhighway is a policing mechanism by which human flesh is gripped in the cyber-jaws of virtualization. The ideology of facilitation? That is the promotional culture of the virtual class which speaks eloquently about how the expansion of the high-speed data network will facilitate every aspect of contemporary society: heightened interactivity, increased high-tech employment in a "globally competitive market," and a massive acceleration of access to knowledge. Not a democratic discourse but a deeply authoritarian one, the ideology of facilitation is always presented in the crisis-context of technological necessitarianism. As the CEO's of leading computer companies and their specialist consultants like to say: *We have no choice but to adapt or perish given the technological inevitability associated with the coming to be of technotopia.* Or, as the virtual elite summarizes the situation: *We will be jettisoned into the history dump file if we don't submit to the imperatives of digital technology.*

Map 4: The Information Elite

Monarchs of the electronic kingdom, the information elite rules the digital superhighway. Having no country except digital-land, no history but for their passing electronic traces, and no future other than the conquest of cyber-culture, the information elite is a global fraternity (mostly male) of data hounds flying the virtual airways. Fueled by missionary enthusiasm for the emergent technologies of technotopia, it is at the empty centre of virtual power.

But like all high priests before them, from the ancient Egyptian ecclesiastics and the Christian Cardinals to the Soviet Commissars, the information elite are practioners of a dead power. A precondition for operating at the centre of any power is the sacred knowledge that power is dead, that its signs are always cynical, and that the price for revealing this secret is expulsion or even death. The information elite lives under the double sign of cynicism and an eternal law of silence. If it should reveal the cynicism within or betray the secret of dead power to the uninitiated its offending member would be executed immediately (or in the twentieth-century version dumped from the virtual class in a classic buyout). Information is a dead sign, and the information elite is the priestly keeper of the eternal flame of the nothingness within.

Map 5: Soft Ideology

> [Nickelodeon's] expansion into preschool territory was part of a larger, marketing strategy for the company. . . "We recognize that if we start getting kids to watch us at this age, we have them for life,". . . "That's exactly the reason why we're doing it." In its fifteen years, Nickelodeon has conquered the marketplace for children between 6 and 11 years old.
>
> *New York Times*, March 21, 1994

Soft TV is the new horizon of the electronic body. An integrated multimedia world where the networks of cyberspace and television suddenly merge into a common telematic language. Cablesoft, Videoway, Smart TV: these are the futuristic (CompuTV) collector points for accessing, harvesting, and distributing the remainders of the virtual body.

Soft TV expresses perfectly the ruling ideology of the virtual class. When the networked world of the information superhighway is finally linked to TV, then the will to virtuality will be free to produce fully functioning networked bodies: cybershoppers, cyberbankers, and cybersex. Soft TV is an electronic televisual space populated by body dumps where human flesh goes to be virtualized. Itself a product of the will to virtuality, soft ideology is necessarily virtual: a series of ruling illusions about the efficacy and inevitability of the virtualization of human experience. Here, the future of the hyper-human body is translated into the language of public policy for immediate circulation through the international networks of political power. Consequently, the soft ideology of the virtual class is based on three key illusions.

The Illusion of Interactivity: Consider Microsoft's newest corporate venture, *Cablesoft*, which is actively promoted under the sign of enhanced interactivity. Cablesoft is a multimedia world linking the programming language of computers with television screens to produce fully integrated media. Cyber-Interactivity is, however, the opposite of *social* relationships. The human presence is reduced to a twitching finger, spastic body, and an oversaturated informational pump that surfs the channels, and makes choices within strictly programmed limits. What is really "interfaced" by Cablesoft, is the soft matter of the brain. It is a standard operating system for melting previously externalized technologies of communication into the human nervous system. And what is the Cablesoft brain? It is multi-platform, multi-media, and multi-disciplinary: a hyper-mind that has its neuro-synapses fired by directly accessed signals drawn from passing data storms on the big bandwidth. The hyper-mind creates tele-consciousness in its wake. Imagine Star Trek's image of the Borg stepping out of the television screen and patching into the Cablesoft mind. Not the interesting ("You will be assimilated") Borg of the early episodes, but the smarmy Borg of the latter episode. The "good Borg" has a veneer of individual consciousness, but an inner reality of suburban consciousness that just wants to do good for the human race. Cablesoft, then, as that point where the individual mind embedded in spinal nerve tissue disappears, and is replaced by *our* circulation as phasal moments in a new medium of cybernetic intelligence. Under the entertainment cover of the ideology of facilitation, Cablesoft promises to mind-meld (our) brains into a circulating process of cyber-intelligence: a total human mind scan for the body electronic.

The Illusion of (Cyber) Knowledge: Soft TV is also sold under the sign of the "knowledge society." Techno-hype has it that wired culture delivers us to a vastly expanded range of human awareness. What is not said, however, is that for the virtual class, true knowledge is cold data, and the very best data of all is the willing read-out of the human sensorium into the info-net. That is why there is such an immense social pressure today for everyone to get on the Net. Unlike the 1950s, with its promotion of technology under the sign of "good industrial design" for consumer society, the 1990s is typified by the glorification of virtual technology under the banner of "good body design" for the cyber-culture of tomorrow. In virtual culture, knowledge is literally vacummed from all the orifices of the body, society, and economy, downloaded into data storage banks, and then sampled and resampled across the liquid media-net, and all this in perfect synch with the expansionary momentum of the recombinant commodity-form. When knowledge is reduced to information, then consciousness is stripped of its lived connection to history, judgment, and experience. What results is the illusion of an expanded knowledge society, and the reality of virtual knowledge. Knowledge, that is, as a tightly controlled medium of cybernetic exchange where thought has a disease, and that disease is called information.

The Illusion of Expanded Choice: Soft TV has a veneer of expanded (consumer) choice, but an inner reality of growing desensitization and infantilization. A multi-channeled world driven by the need for information by all the drifting cyber-minds projects itself perfectly by the promise of 500 channel television. A channel for every firing synapse, a data stream for every retro-mood. If there can be such intense demand for quantum leaps of televisual information ports for the hungry cablesoft brain it is because the cyber-mind has already patched to a new emotional territory. Not expansive minds for expanded (Soft TV) choice, but a fantastic infantilization of the televisual audience, with its fever pitch connections between (emotional) primitivism and (multi-media) hyper-tech. Why the charismatic appeal today of scandal TV and talk-show formats privileging the deterioration of the public mind? It is because virtual culture has already evolved into a new, more insidious phase of nihilism: that moment where self-hatred and self-abuse is so sharp that we willingly deliver ourselves up as the butt of the TV joke. The cultural condition that makes this possible is that, like the training programs for CIA assassins with their repeated exposure of agents to brutal scenes of torture, Soft TV functions on the basis of desensitization. Floating corpses, live executions, rape TV: all delivered under the sign of media fascination, and all with the intent of desensitizing the soft mass of the cyber-audience to the point of its humiliated complicity in the evil of the times.

Map 6: The Red Guard Meets Generation X

The editors of AXCESS magazine, published in San Diego, recently wrote about themselves as the "young entrepreneurs": the leading-edge members of Generation X. At about the same time, a CBC TV program, entitled "Red Capitalism," interviewed former members of the Red Guard who have now become full-fledged participants of the rising Chinese entrepreneurial class. So what happens when the old ideological competition between capitalism and socialism disappears, and Generation X meets the Red Guard on the world stage, they look in the mirror of shared economic interests, and discover to their pleasant surprise that they are exactly the same (virtual) class? Perhaps this fusion of unlikely partners in a global virtual class of young entrepreneurs who are finally liberated from Cold War ideology was best expressed by a high-ranking official at the Boeing Company when asked about the linkage of human rights issues with the extension of "most favored nation" status to China. He argued that there should be no relationship between politics and trade: "We are living in the age of global competition." Without a twinge of nostalgia for the disappeared rhetoric of "jobs for Americans," the official from Boeing is joined in this chorus for unimpeded free trade by multinational corporate leaders (think of the American multinational directors in China who castigated the U.S. Secretary of State for criticizing the Chinese record on human rights) and government officials (the Canadian Minister for External Affairs has recently announced a new public policy in relations with Latin- and South America whereby trade is cut loose from human rights issues). A fundamental political objective of the virtual class is decoupling the linkage between free trade (virtualized exchange) and human rights. That is why the technotopians of Generation X and the ex-cadres of the Red Guard are hyper-linked by the same ideology. With the death of communism, the world has undergone a big political flip. In the glory days of the Cold War, business would have justified its expansionary interests in the name of fighting the Red Menace. Today the virtual class valorizes its recombinant interests in the name of emancipating business from the shackles of (Cold War) political rhetoric. Like meaning before it, human rights issues slow down the rate of circulation of virtualized exchange, and, consequently, they must be eliminated from the political history file.

The 1990s, therefore, are typified by the rapid decline of the hard ideologies of capitalism and communism, and by the ascendancy of the soft ideology of the virtual class. Soft ideology? That's the will to virtuality as the common language of the new managerial elites of the post-capitalist, post-communist, and also post-technological society.

Itself a product of the will to virtuality, soft ideology is necessarily virtual: a series of ruling illusions about the efficacy and inevitability of the virtualization of experience. Here, the future of the hyperhuman body is translated into the language of public policy for immediate circulation through the international networks of political power. When the Red Guard meets the (technotopian) members of Generation X on the common ground of missionary enthusiasm for pan-capitalism, they insert themselves into the political economy of virtual reality as its leading elites. As the young entrepreneurs of Generation X, the virtual class finally has a name. Under the sign of the Red Guard gone technotopian, it also has an historical destiny—creating a new global "cultural revolution" on behalf of unimpeded virtualized exchange. Finally, in the fusion of the young entrepreneurs of Generation X and the Red Guard, it has a grisly political method: sacrificing human rights at the altar of virtual (economic) expediency. We're living in the new morning of a big (ideological) sign-switch. The Cold War of hard ideology may finally be over, but the new Cold War of soft ideology, the one that pits the virtual class against all barriers to its global sovereignty, is just beginning.

CHAPTER TWO

Virtual Ideology
or the cultural logic of the
recombinant sign

Virtual ideology? That's the event horizon of our coming transformation into high density fibre-optic flesh. Consider the crash robotic performances of Stelarc: the Australian (by way of Japan) performance artist who has made of his mutating body a radical experiment in redesigning the flesh for cruising the Net at hyper-speeds. Stelarc's philosophy is explicit: the human body as we have known it has reached an evolutionary dead-end. It has stopped adapting to major changes in cyber-culture, and has flat-lined at its usurpation by the bio-genetics of virtual reality. For Stelarc, unless the flesh is radically refitted for virtual life in the fast lane, it will be left behind, an inert cultural residue floating in history, witness to late twentieth-century nostalgia for the body organic. His challenge: to reskin the body with synthetic flesh that will cover the miniature nano-gear jammed inside and serve as a photosynthesizing agent for energizing the body telematic. His ideal body image necessitates dumping the body wetware into the cultural shredder, filling its cavities with techno-organs, microscopic sensors for quick detection of approaching breakdowns in the body's vital functions. Eyes, ears and taste must be amplified, making of the sensory orifices a brilliant graphical interfacing system for quick talk with all the environing imaging-machines. People wince when Stelarc talks this way, and they certainly cringe in dead-eyed fascination as they watch his body-robotic performances, especially the one in which his eyes are jacked into CPU

Intel chips, his flesh hardwired to an awesome bank of Sun system computer optics, and the CO_2 emissions of his internal respiratory organs are filtered through android sampler machines to create the screaming thunder music of the body rasping, creaking and groaning as it is displaced into the algorithmic array of digital reality.

But Stelarc is right. The body future will either *be recombinant* or it will disappear into a terminal evolutionary exit. Trapped in the violent force-field of virtual reality, cyber-flesh is our telematic horizon. And why be surprised? Reports are coming back that hackers prowling the night alleys of cyber-outlawland in Washington, D.C. have adopted the battle cry: "We want to be machines." A throaty roar of approval for the telematic vision of dumping the body biological into virtualization, and calling it nano-freedom. A deadly mixture of humiliated flesh and a raw sense of inferiority before the pulsating imaging-system of virtual reality. Virtual ideology, then, as the body wetware on a lonely, but no less ecstatic, road trip across the pixel-starred electronic sky of the cyber-net. Consequently, an end to the simulacrum, and the beginning of cyber-bodies; an eclipse of nostalgia for the body organic, and the ascendancy of a violent resurrection-effect of the body telematic as a recombinant sign of its own disappearance. The next millennium spreads out before us as a fatal scene where things disappear only to the extent that they are more (virtually) present than ever before. And not just things, but the third millennium itself has already disappeared under the weight of future-boredom, and will only make one final appearance as a resurrection-effect of the next 1000 years as raw material for VR generators. Cloning, splicing, transcribing, resequencing: that is the sound of the digital future as only more electronic data for the (virtual) history file.

So, then, ten theses on the cultural logic of the recombinant sign as the ruling ideology of virtual reality:

Thesis 1: The Recombinant Sign

Virtual ideology operates like this. At the centre of virtual reality is the *recombinant sign*: this sub-human strike weapon, what Bruce Sterling described as the "military-entertainment complex", has as its aim the recuperation of "virtuality as a strategic asset" (Sterling again). Its "product" is the creation of process bodies fit for cutting and pasting across the telematic space of virtual reality. The recombinant sign displays a (post)historical ambition in archiving every element of human experience into a densely layered, relational data-base. Its overall political method consists in the transformation of the technological media of communication into a pure cybernetic system. Its economic base is constituted by intensifiying the recombinant commodity-form until it finally explodes beyond the domain of political economy, launching itself in a brilliant stellar blast as the new global astronomy of the recombinant sign. The most advanced expression possible of the will to virtuality, the recombinant sign is pure ideology. It is also a mutating bio-cybernetic apparatus that embodies in its controlling logic (recursive and teleonomic) the world-view of the technological class; that channels process economy into process bodies; that eddies wildly like a gigantic weather system alternating between moving (cold) fronts of technological euphoria and (warm) fronts of primitivism; and that interpellates the recombinant commodity with the virtualized remainder of reclining flesh. The recombinant sign is how flesh is most deeply hooked by pan-capitalism.

Thesis 2: Cynical Seduction

The recombinant sign is the purest expression possible of cynical culture. Here, all the old referents of cultural experience are reduced to a degree-zero: the content of contemporary culture is irrelevant, except as a virtual hook to attract the attention of bodies in recline or for the more strategic purpose of inculcating infantilization as the elemental political (pre)condition for recombinant culture. The fabled "audience-commodity" is transformed into a passive, yet highly active, relational relay in the larger circuitry of wired culture. Refusing the doubled logic of cultural manipulation and repressive desublimation, and abandoning the viewpoint of culture as epiphenomenon of (product) economy (which no longer exists), the recombinant sign initiates the era of *cynical seduction*. What energizes the system, animating its virtual rendering of the social in recline, is the recursive cultural logic of the parallel processsing of opposites (TV news where opposing story lines are intended to be cancel each other out), and quick (media) flips and sudden (advertising) reversals (a whole promotional culture that can now publicize scenes of reproductive harmony because we are safely in the age of the virtualized body). Always cynical, the recombinant sign privileges only process: process bodies, entertainment, news, "attention," and catastrophes. Having only an antagonistic interest in local space (except for the forays into cultural nostalgia by the laser vectors of the media scanning system), and being culturally allergic to bounded culture, the recombinant sign works the logic of cynical seduction in its fibre-optic axes in dead space, dead culture, and dead imaging-repertoires.

Thesis 3: Information(less) Economy for Screenal Bodies

No longer the age of the information economy, the recombinant sign functions to destroy the relationship between meaning and communication. A born enemy of the technological media of "communication," the recombinant sign sets in motion a cultural economy drained of media (as simulacra of communication) and bleached of meaning, like the skeletal remains of dead cattle under the withering desert sun in all those faded westerns. Meaning slows down process bodies, acting as a circuit-breaker in the circulatory movements of cyber-culture. It must be destroyed, and it is. Perfectly cybernetic, the recombinant sign hovers at the event-horizon of the information(less) economy: a deep space worm that sucks into its imploding spirals all the detrital matter of reclining culture. Finally freed of the inertial drag of social meaning and having warp-jumped over the densely accrued mass of (social) communication, the recombinant sign can become what it always wanted to be, but never could (in the age of technology as communication): a cultural microchip that speeds up the passing (virtual) scene to mega-overdrive, recodes the human species into an elliptical game of simulation, and burns down remaining signs of intelligent life (lurking in embodied flesh) into a brilliant flare-out that spreads its terminal signature-pattern across the digital sky. For the recombinant commodity, information checkmates process, and it must be vectorized.

Thesis 4: Tattooed Retinas

Nissan's television advertisement, "Built for the Human Race," is a particularly vicious gateway to the twenty-first century. Its double meaning of the human race as species-logic and crash speed is perfect: a (technological) true confession as a big lie. Technologies are no longer built for the human species, but the human race has been genetically engineered as a phasal moment in the cybernet. Nissan's TV ad is our tele-history where talking means the telephone, listening MTV, neighborhoods a freeway exit, reading renting a video or listening to an audio book on the car tape when lost in gridlock, geography a node on the Internet, cities global grid positions processed by vectors of movement, friends TV families like *Cheers*, working "growing a business," social life networking, and politics selling an image-repertoire. The will to technology is about the will to virtuality, and the will to virtuality is about the business of *growing a human race*: a bio-technical species for spooling and slipstreaming through the vectoral spaces and nodes of the cybernet.

The 1990s are (culturally) fascinating and (politically) grim because the key movements of the recombinant history of the next millennium are being swiftly put into place. The old ideologies of socialism and capitalism have quickly been deleted from the virtual history file, and the electronic frontier of pan-capitalism is taking their place. Like that other American (software) frontier that was built to the background noise of railways (hardware) colonizing space, the electronic frontier opens for an instant, only to be immediately colonized by those new (cybernetic) railroads: the recombinant commodity-form (pan-capitalism), the recombinant sign (virtual culture), and recombinant history (the virtual memory spools of the next century). *Genie, Prodigy, Compuserve, Virtual Vision, Micros*oft: the names say it all. The (virtual) logic of the next century is already deeply inside us, and we are the recombinant bodies built for the telematic race.

And our Nissan future? It's this: virtual reality as the genetic engineering of a new "technical beast" (Thurow) programmed by (American) software, equipped by (Japanese) hardware, and aestheticized by (European) wetware. Either electronic technology has got to get its feet wet by entering the bag of water and bones that is the human body, or the skin has to be dried out: flopping like a fish out of water and "gasping for air on the shores of a drying lake" (Grant). The will to virtuality provides a pragmatic compromise: technology that comes inside the skin in the form of nano-chips, miniaturised digital submarines that float in the blood stream. The body is drained of its drag-weight of water, lasered by technologies from photography and television to cellular phones and computers. Invaded from the outside by nano-technology and exterior-ized from within by hyper-imaging systems, the body is ready to be dumped into the virtual matrix.

Welcome to the millennium: a non-time of tattooed retinas, phrack skins, recursive nerves, and object-oriented (programmed) brains.

Thesis 5: The Second American Civil War

In the bondage rituals of pan-capitalism, culture is not a reflex of the recombinant commodity (energy), but the recombinant sign (bio-signification) coordinates the cybernetic chain of hierarchical con-trol. No longer a materialist culture (that vanished long ago into the imaging-system), nor culture as a simple chain of signification (language is now only a fading metaphor for organic technology that has not yet learned how to speak), but culture as a cybernetic system: recombinant, semiurgical, and immensely vital because it long ago ceased to have a real, material body. In recombinant culture, dead signs trump material energy because this is a culture of disappearances, populated by screenal bodies.

And why not? The recombinant sign is all about fighting the *second* American Civil War, but this time on a global (cultural) scale. In the original Civil War, Grant and Sherman quickly proved themselves the leading Generals of Virtual America. Unlike the locally bounded gener-als of the old South--Lee and Stonewall Jackson most of all--Grant and Sherman understood that war is waged for virtual space: a vectored battle for positions across a floating (Southern) space. Relational (in its kill ratios), circulatory and fluid in its flanking movements, exterminist in its logic, virtual war is driven by the promotional (war) culture of cynical sacrifice. The South was doomed from the beginning because it chose the wrong answer in a physics test: it chose territorial possession (classical mechanical energy), and thus was bound in a bunkered, serialized space with no degrees of freedom. The North, probably thinking ahead to a happy, hegemonic future of the American postmodern, had already flipped into virtualized space, with its industrialized eye on the coloniza-tion of the western lands. A struggle over a quantum physics (of virtual war) waiting to be born in the heat of battle, the Civil War fused American paternity rites to the genealogy of the recombinant sign.

Now that the original Civil War casts a thousand last lives in nostalgic (televisual) reprises, a second American Civil War is already being waged across the global grid of recombinant culture. It is fought in two theaters: as a *virtual war* programmed by the military-entertainment complex and as a *virtual culture* uplinked by the universal media class. The same privileging of virtual space that dominated the strategical thinking of Grant and Sherman (and the primitive, biblical dreams of Lincoln) is the animating spirit of the new American military-entertainment matrix. When the American military lost sight of the lessons in virtuality of the Civil War and went to ground in energy (territorial possession of localized space) in Vietnam, they promptly lost the war. For the real (cybernetic) lessons of Vietnam, read Bruce Sterling's brilliant account of "Virtual War" (*Wired*), in which he describes the virtual reality battles of the Gulf War. His account includes cyber-Colonels, straight from the defeated past of Vietnam, who study intently in War College a strobed-array of multi-media computer simulations of the "Battle of East Lansing", an axial coordinate in the Iraqi desert where heat-seeking missiles in a blinding storm vaporized a large Iraqi heavy-tank corps. Or consider Sterling's bitterly insightful reflections, after spending time at the the main military-industrial security conference in Austin, on the euphoric merger of Silicon Valley and the Pentagon around the key concept of "virtuality as a strategic asset." According to him, Virtual War has already begun, and the coming conquest will belong to the recombinant power which grafts a logistics of (global, scanning) perception to the holy grail of fibre-optic weaponry.

Not only is the virtualization of military culture under way, but the colonization of the globe is achieved by downloading American culture into the expectant orifices of local territorial space. It is not only the technological class that is against the working class, but a universal media class that is arrayed against local populations. This universal media class is also engaged in a virtual war of cultural positionality, exterminism (of memoried culture), sacrifice (to an endless circulation of the "new"): perfectly co-relational (in its media practices), co-extensive (in its cultural consciousness), and co-spatialized (in its liquidation of durational time). For this class, new organs without body type are created for vectoring across the dead, ether zone of the universal media archive. The flesh is burnt hyper-red (from too many hours under the hot klieg lights), the brain can sustain only nano-second attention spans, and no principled (fixed, territorial) political positions exist. As Nietzsche, probably thinking about the vacuumed android skulls of TV announcers, said: "Fence straddlers. They sit in the middle. That is what their smirking tells us."

It no longer matters that America is disappearing into its own after-image. That only speeds up the rate of cultural transmission, and makes the sign of dead America an object of dead fascination. Necrophilia as the ruling cultural tendency of clonal societies. The cultural genotype of America has long ago been retrobased from its spinal ganglia of nerves, sequenced, and transferred around the world to all the waiting cultural geno-banks. Not even clonal cultures, but monstrous hybrids: Euro/ Disney, Amer/Japan, Amer/China. America can finally disappear because its (historical) memory has been filed in the universal media archive. Like the remains of a dying red star, only the endlessly blinking pulsar of violence in the circulatory arteries of the U.S.A. remains as a sign of the galactic implosion that marked America's final disappearance. It's the American Century: the end of all centuries where the American cultural code becomes the world hologram, and the national space that was America remains behind as a scene of detrital, but for that matter no less fascinating, violence.

Schwarzkopf in Vietnam: A Soldier Returns. One last lingering (CBS) image: General Schwarzkopf revisits "Saigon" with that other TV warrior—Dan Rather—and, like two old vets visiting Civil War grave-yards, they look over the now peaceable kingdom of the bucolic Vietnamese battleground and opine. Schwarzkopf, with cynical piety: "Killing people is never fun." And Rather cynically asks: "Did they all die in vain?" To which the General responds: "No, it happened, that's all. It is part of our development as a nation." America as the owner of full TV rights to the long-running serial: *Vietnam: The Rerun.*

Thesis 6: Cyber-Hooks

All the glittering flotsam of contemporary culture consists of cyber-hooks for grappling and boarding the electronic body. Virtualized flesh threatens to vanish into a pure simulation (of itself). Accordingly, it must be slowed and forced to leave body signs of its silent, swift passing on the quivering registers of the cultural bubble chambers. And there are a lot of bubble chambers these days: TV for capturing the invisible photons of the eye electronic, radio for scanning the digitized register of the ear mutant, computers for registering in their cold numberical codes the presence and disappearance of invisible neutrinos of vectored intelligence, and MTV for finally proving that an audience never existed for a music that only had a combinatorial logic. The media, therefore, express poignantly, but smilingly, the awful pathos of electronic culture: futile efforts, but no less courageous for all their mindlessness, to slow the electronic body, and to prove to the last beneficiaries of pan-capitalism that it all meant something, that something was real, that someone was here, if only in the fatigued form of virtualized exchange. Some urine on a wall in a vacant alley at dusk.

Thesis 7: From Digital Badlands to the Virtual Cafe

The recombinant sign speaks the language of virtualized imaging-systems. Press the delete key and the obsolescent critical rhetorics of cultural studies (nostalgic ressentiment), semiology (discursive analysis which cannot penetrate the electronic cloud cover of the bio-apparatus), cultural sociology (society is the missing matter of virtual reality), and dialectical materialism (for a culture that is recursive and virtual in its cybernetic logic) vanish from the screen, to be filed away in the theory in ruins data base. Segue to the copy function and suddenly the high-density pixel screen is windowed by graphic images of the body recombinant, straight from dead-end outlaw canyons scattered around the digital badlands. Hyper-human bodies zoom and drift across the zone of sub-nature in the ether-net. A slacker's body which does not seem to have much to do, endlessly refracts its virtualized image into mirrored fractals, digitally coded by a highly specific geometry of mathematical coordinates and illustrated with mutating and vibrant skin tones.

The electronic body of the recombinant sign is a wonderful space of illusion: filtered images, displaced sounds, morphed faces, aliased eyes, a time-stretched nervous system, and cut and paste sexuality. Knowing no real, the electronic body is always ready to travel across the galactic space of the hyperreal. Having no vestigial memory of nature, the body electronic thinks of itself as sub-nature, a world of sub-reality that creates its own laws of motion on the virtual go. Never having felt desire, the virtualized flesh dreams of a fantasy palace: a lasered space of sexuality without a ground, of temptation without resistance, of desire spinning away into a relational net of discharged electronic affect. Always poised at the cyber-edge of spasm and crash, virtualized flesh can finally know itself as a pacific dreamland of violent irruptions: flickering from red to blue in the color spectrum as it searches for an infinite (technical) perfection that it will never attain. Its telematic fate? To disappear in the bad infinity of an image that is in a state of (virtual) grace because it is means after means. No longer an "evil demon of images," but the recombinant sign as the will to purity. Pure images that shed the dirty materialism of street culture as they whirl away into a combinatorial matrix of dead signs. Electrolyte blue eyes, shock green hair, and a third sex for hanging out with other (genetically-engineered) body-constructs at the Virtual Cafe.

Thesis 8: Advertising as the Highest Stage of (Recombinant) Art in the Age of Pan-Capitalism

Advertisements are sunshine reports for reclining flesh. The body electronic finds its mirrored double in their panoramic, but frenzied, scans of the crash body as it moves from flesh to virtuality. Not scenes of a future yet to unfold, but of a semiurgical, virtual past that the electronic body has already experienced. Certainly not a machinery of solicitation for manipulable masses, but a bio-apparatus of dissuasion for virtualized flesh. A "strange attractor," advertising is a massive defensive armature created by the mediascape to win back virtualized flesh to the logistics of desire. However, the bio-net of advertising must fail because the body electronic has already vectored along the vapor trail of virtual reality, leaving behind only a brilliant, because ghostly, halo-effect marking its disappearance from earthly space.

That halo-effect is the machinery of advertising: sign-posts marking the exit of the body from the noosphere of the organic flesh. Regressive yet projective, anxious yet serene, nostalgic yet hyperreal, advertising is like a plasmic bio-net arching across the invisible skin of the virtualized body as it follows its destiny to crash speed. The electronic archive of advertising is filled with the detritus of the crash body: the jettisoned remains of dead fetishes, dead desire and dead objects. The emblematic electronic marker of the end of the twentieth-century body, advertising is about failure. Enchanting because it is so deeply inertial, the advertising net tries to recapture the disappearing body on behalf of pan-capitalism. To fill the body electronic with radium trace elements, sometimes fluids (beer), at other times to tinker with its mechanics (cars), to play with its desire (the imaging-system for dead sex), or to puzzle over its liquid wastes (diaper commercials): anything will be promo-ed for the virtual body to register on the fading screenal economy of pan-capitalism. Like Barthes's iron filings cast across an invisible magnetic field to mark the passage of the disappearing sign, advertising is the will to make its vanishing mass visible, and thus risible, to the promotional culture of pan-capitalism.

But the virtual body will not be fooled. It already exists on the other dark side of the end of advertising. If its internal circadian rhythms of electronic sex, desire, appetites, and fetishes register on the scoping scanners of the advertising bio-net, that is because it is the (virtual) world's first aesthetic practitioner of the trompe-l'oeil. Advertsing is, then, a gestural game of ruse and counter-ruse as virtualized flesh plays with the gravitational pressure of sign-objects, and the machinery of advertising sets ever more alluring electronic snares to capture in its inertial trap the floating orifices of the electronic body. Not the ancient fable of the hare and the tortoise, but the virtual enigma of the circuit-breaker (of pan-capitalism) and the crash body. Always a struggle between the debt liquidation cycle of reclining flesh (the fall into the heavy weight of advertising) and the over-heated, hyper-inflated virtual economy of Crash. In an age infected by the will to purity, advertising is a fall into sin from the virtual state of grace.

Thesis 9: Jurassic America

Jurassic Park, the movie, attracts such immense fascination because it operates psychologically as a vast "screen-effect," registering in displaced televisual form our own anxieties and fears over the extinction of the human species.

Like the northern cod (over-fished), buffalo and carrier pigeons (over-hunted), and ancient rain forests (over-clearcut), the human species is also on the verge of extinction, a victim of over-virtualization.

Overwhelmed by rapid improvements in the ability of technology to harvest the human species, the organic body no longer can reproduce itself quickly enough as its energies are drained away by a relentless series of over-virtualizations moving at the speed of (TV) light: *over-virtualized food* (the contamination of the ecological chain by the chemical retrobasing of processed food); *over-virtualized weather* (sunburns in the winter as ozone in the atmosphere is leaked away by NASA rocket launches), *over-virtualized skin* (the X-raying of the body by the terminals of the screenal economy), over-virtualized orifices, from eyes and ears to the floating nose (as the imaging-systems of virtual reality come inside us, and we become the body combinatorial of digital reality), and even *over-virtualized lungs* (from the dead oxygen of cigarettes to the dead air of passenger jets radiating us through the stratosphere). Harvested by the will to virtuality, the human species suddenly disappears into an imaging-system that always operates cannibalistically (McLuhan). Here, the externalization of the central nervous system into technological media of communication represents the primal act of technology eating human flesh, consuming the human species and calling it entertainment.

As body organs disappear into the virtual rendering machines of digital reality, the human species relives its anthropological past one more time at those fabulous theme parks that are created for the preservation of the tourist DNA of extinct species. From the cinema of Jurassic Park to Disney's America, a televisual world, then, of theme parks for the study of the human species as a post-species: virtual death. No longer the creation of federally-protected wilderness zones (for preserving the DNA of extinct nature) or the policing of No-Fish zones on the Grand Banks (for archiving surviving schools of extinct fish-lines), but now the mandating of No-Harvesting zones for post-humans: televisual theme parks that are strictly off-limits to normal business, because their real business is the study of (our) disappearance. A characteristic feature of the human species as a post-species is that its surviving members like to revisit the sites of their virtual extinction played out in the televisual world of promotional culture. Jurassic Park, then, as alternatively reopening the wound of our vanishing into virtual reality, and the more ancient (dinosaur) pattern of retracing the route of (our) disappearance. Cynical nostalgia as the key psychology of the post-species of the sub-human that burns out in a blaze of sacrificial mimesis.

Thesis 10: The Lonely (Virtual) Crowd

The "virtual community" of electronic networking has such charismatic appeal today because, like a failing spacecraft, we are re-entering the burning atmosphere of the lonely (virtual) crowd. Not David Riesman's famous image of the "lonely crowd" written for America in the modern century, but now lonely telematic individuals huddled around terminal event-scenes (computer screens, TV sets, high-performance stereos) willing themselves to become members of a virtual community. A technologically generated community that has no existence other than as a perspectival simulacrum, and on behalf of which the media-net functions as a violent, but always technically perfectible force-field (the "perfect sound," "more memory capacity") for hiding the loneliness within. The appeal of electronic networking operates in inverse proportion to the disconnectedness of people from each other, of the recombinant sign from the human species, and of the body digitized from the abandoned site of the organic body. Consequently, the ruling ideological formula of virtual culture: electronic mediation at the (recombinant) top; organic disconnection from below.

The lonely, virtual crowd has its casualties. Consider two cultural event-scenes: first, the movie, *Falling Down,* in which white suburban anxiety about the violence and inertia of the virtual city (L.A.), is discharged into cinematic vengeance-taking on the streets. Here, Nietzsche's aphorism that "someone must be to blame for my feeling ill" has its denouement in the lonely anti-hero who breaks free from the electronic crowd (the endless traffic jam), and goes to sacrificial ground in scenes of rough justice. The moral lesson: those who dare to leave (technological) gridlock fall immediately into a Hobbesian state of nature, where only the predatory beast within prevails.

Second, consider that virtual moment when *Falling Down* comes off the movie screen, and like a strange shape-shifter assumes human form in the person of Gian Luigi Ferri, the broker who killed six people and wounded six others in a San Francisco law office before he committed suicide. Described as a "very gentle, very friendly, a chubby little guy...[who] was hard up. [H]e was hurting," Ferri went to battle armed with three semi-automatic pistols and orange ear protectors. Why? Nobody knows. A broker, probably caught in the debt liquidation cycle,

Ferri reportededly often sat alone in his car, outside his deserted office in a strip mall. Was he seeking revenge for his financial ruin? Maybe. Or was he the American version of Sartre's "pure existential act": violence without motive? In this case, Ferri could be read as a doubled sign of the lonely (virtual) individual: a sign of the predictable cultural fallout from the violence of the recombinant commodity as it sweeps its deflationary way through real-estate markets. Ferri is also the quintessential cultural expression of the Hobbesian departure from the lonely (virtual) crowd: the vengeance-seeking skyscraper warrior who transforms spurious fantasies and depressive anxiety into a violent discharge of affect onto the public (law office) situation. Mr. Virtuality sits in his car on a lonely San Francisco afternoon, plotting his revenge. In his person, the deflationary cycle of the recombinant commodity meets the expansionary momentum of the recombinant sign, and the result is mass murder.

The proof of this: in his suicide note which was found the next day, Ferri justified his actions by a doubled logic: first, in terms of the recombinant commodity, by attacking lawyers as contemporary "esquires" (in the Middle Ages, esquires "roamed the countryside to steal from working people and give to the prince"); and secondly, in terms of the recombinant sign, by denouncing the "poison in our cells" ("The last thing that made all of this come to a head is that I am one of those people of the 5% of the population where the poison monosodium glutamate (MSG) has reached such high levels in our cells, that a minium amount more can kill us" (*New York Times*, July 4, 1993).

Happy 4th of July from hell, then, from a street-messenger of the lonely (virtual) crowd.

CHAPTER THREE

The Will to Virtuality
The Recline of the West

Death of the Spasm Priests

The present age is one of protracted, perhaps interminable, recline. Nietzsche's prediction that we would see ascetic priests and blinking wonders at the end (that may never end) has come true, only the latter have proven to turn vicious under stress and become fascists. The ascetic priests, though, never change, being necessary to all regimes whatever their ideologies.

Recline is the strategy of declining life. Weakening life increasingly needs more and more prosthetics. For invalid life, culture is reduced to a standing reserve of prosthetic devices. Declining life creates a cultural cocoon around itself, a virtuality, part imaginary and part technology, with ever more tenuous connections to the vanishing (vanished?) "life-world." The secret of Nietzsche's "last man" is the will to virtuality, the will to surrender oneself to technologically-mediated and externalized imaginaries. Meanwhile the flesh gets scanned and processed through machines in a waiting period before it gets replaced by fully fabricated organisms, that is, pure virtual intentionalities for a virtual world. We begin to doubt that there are any ascetic priests. Who did we have in mind? Michael Jackson? Recline is post-Nietzschian. Indulgence is total. No one is administering recline. General thesis: A process of recline into virtuality is interrupted by (frequent) spasms of fascism and is possibly a cover for a crash that may have already taken place. Indeed, it is immaterial whether or not the crash has occurred: recline proceeds as if it were a crash-effect, behaves as if the struggle is over and that we are the dying on an abandoned battlefield seeking whatever comfort might be possible in our last moments. We exist in the interim between the human and its extinction or replacement. That makes us post-human, but not yet unhuman.

The age of the human was dominated by the ideological objective of realizing one or another conception of human essence. The post-human age is ruled by the wish, mostly unconscious, to replace the human. There are innumerable covers for that wish, objectives that fall short of its maximum fulfillment, the most pervasive being the will to virtuality and the sacrificial will of fascism, the remnants of the bi-modern after the ascetic priests have disappeared.

Interminability

The ideology of recline is interminability. It begins within modernism when Peirce declares the interminability of science and Freud announces the (possible) interminability of analysis. Nietzsche sees through (to) this and proclaims the eternal return as a challenge to recline: what is interminable is a process of *repetition*. He did not foresee that his insight would be enacted in the twentieth century as "retread culture." Nietzsche's challenge has been ignored by successive generations of recliners whose ideologues have found ways to delay the inevitable. Rorty's endless conversation, Lyotard's indefinite drifting, Derrida's empirical wandering (interminable deconstruction), Habermas's ideal speech community are the latest efforts to blink away, through reaction formation. We continue for the sake of continuing and in the hope that some (technological) miracle might happen that would "save" everything. That hope, of course, is purely cynical. We all know unconsciously, if not reflexively, that every "advance" of technological regulation is another stage in our replacement. On the surface we find interminability, beneath it is the will to virtuality, and beneath that is the wish to be replaced, the form that the death-wish takes in an age that lives by and for Culture, because Culture (the sign-world and its technological extensions) has weakened life to the point at which life is too *intimidated* by it even to try to control it. Things like the war machine and its domestic counterpart the medical machine are two ways of wreaking havoc on the flesh. Toxic chemicals are another. Hence, bodies recline into virtuality under the reassuring reaction formation of interminability: there is always more time, "it" never ends. On the other hand, every particular thing ends, including that particular construction-thing, the "human race." The human race has probably already crashed, but as crash-effects we have suffered a stroke that leaves us relatively unaware that the world has become a hospice. We are, as Nietzsche suggested, terminally ill. That is why our postmodern ideology is interminability: "I could stay here forever talking with you." The attitude of people hanging out at McDonald's: the ideal speech community which is already there, but is overlooked by "critical theory."

Modernism and postmodernism are the two great ideological phases of recline. An example of each will track the process. Take Georg Lukács in his pre-Marxist period to illustrate modernism. In his *Theory of the Novel* Lukács argues that the totality of social life has been destroyed in the modern world. The novel as a literary form reflects de-totalization. G.H.R. Parkinson summarizes: "Whereas the epic poem gives form to a totality which is self-enclosed [the Greek polis as romanticized by Lukács], the novel seeks to discover and construct a totality of life that is now hidden."[1] The *dédoublement*, however, does not succeed, so "the novel expresses the insight that meaning can never wholly penetrate reality." Yet the novelist "sees that the distinction between subject and object is abstract and limited, and has a glimpse of a unified world." All of this is what Derrida can't swallow, what postmodernists have to reject, what they can't include: nostalgia. Here is evidence of early recline, in which the patient is making fitful moves to get out of bed and making noises about getting back to work that are not meant to be taken seriously by anyone including the performer of the charade. Already in modernism transcendence of the de-totalized has become a cynical sign: the "seeker," as Lukács calls the novel's protagonist, cannot believe in unity but keeps pursuing its idea. Someone who has recently lost a limb still feels that limb until the nervous system adjusts. Modernism is the state of feeling and at last of merely wanting to feel the phantom organ of totality. The "honest seeker" is not searching at all, but is staying in bed and playing with a de-totalization effect. That game ends with the Camusian "absurd," the Sartrian "useless passion," and Heidegger's "listening for Being."

Take Franco Moretti, a post-Marxist, to illustrate postmodernism. In his discussion of the novel, Moretti notes that it is based on conversation, which is never binding or irrevocable, and which "suspends action (symptomatically, a conversation can 'go on forever')": "Conversation creates an easy and indecisive no-man's land between subject and object, protecting both from too-deep probings with the conventions of good manners, and giving voice to the slow worldly process by which characters shape themselves in coming to terms with their society."[2] Here is the second phase of recline on the plane of ideology. Moretti contrasts the novel's indefiniteness to the "moment of truth" in tragedy, calling belief in the latter as a political commitment an "unhealthy complicity of melodrama and emptiness." Postmodernism prefers to be novelistic, drifting in "the no-man's land between subject and object." As against the Marxist Lukács's doctrine that "the economic crisis acts precisely as capitalism's moment of truth," post-Marxist Moretti recurs to "Politics as a Vocation," "an old speech by Max Weber, from which there is probably still a lot to learn" (such as the "ethic of responsibility"): "No tragic yearning for catastrophe as the well-spring of truth, then: no metaphysical contempt for 'consequences', no Baroque delight in 'exception.'"[3] Recline as a series of negations. Nostalgia for totality is over and done with: the novel (life) is no longer structured by *irony* as it was for Lukács, but by compromise, "'half-truth': the form truth takes when it accepts a *compromise with life*." Recline as the spurious safety of compromise, laced with the "good European's" bromide that acceptance of the novelistic "need not lead to unending humiliations and compromises."

Nostalgia for Weberian heroism remains. Weber, however, believed that the great test of modern life would be the challenge to bear up to the insignificance of mundanity. For Moretti, mundanity is not a challenge but a haven from sacrificial politics. He has entered the hospice of postmodernity with a case of terminal interminability, a retro-Weberian acting under the cynical sign of "responsibility." Searching gives way to coping. Have a little Havelism.

Virtual Reality/Retro-Fascism

The ideology of interminability, which unites *all* trends of thought in contemporary discursive space (including Gadamer's hermeneutics,

Althusser's scientific Marxism, Derrida's deconstruction, Rorty's liberalism, Habermas's humanism), is an enormous sign of denial, a reaction formation against acknowledgment of all the Baudrillardian "deaths" (society, history, all the substitution-signs for God). This ideology is also a denial of Crash, of the condition of being *interim*, not interminable. The lead rocket, Humanity, and all of its formation have crashed: antihumanism is a *fact*, a condition, not a position. Something better than the flesh has seduced and intimidated it, the technological imaginary — virtual reality. The imaginary materializes through and in technology, its most privileged form being the hyper-real. Heard at an academic meeting: a good use for virtual reality would be to make sex offenders experience the sufferings of their victims. A whole new penology opens up, topping the panopticon. Soon torture will become (virtual) torture-effects. Think of a system of home imprisonment in which the convicts live engrafted in VR suits that place them within perpetually punitive environments. A modern Dante wouldn't write poetry, but would be a corrections engineer.

In "The Work of Art in the Age of Mechanical Reproduction," Walter Benjamin provided a remarkably precise description of hyper-space and hyper-reality in his discussion of the relation between the technological apparatus of film-making and its resulting product: "in the studio the mechanical equipment has penetrated so deeply into reality [substitute "the scenario"] that its pure aspect freed from the foreign substance of equipment is the result of a special procedure, namely the shooting by the specially adjusted camera and the mounting of the shot together with similar ones. The equipment-free aspect of reality [the scenario] here has become the height of artifice; the sight of immediate reality [the equipment-free scenario] has become an orchid in the land of technology."[4] We can expand upon Benjamin's insight to understand virtual reality-effects. Turn the scenario into a projected imaginary that constitutes a total sensory environment and one has the formal perfection of virtual reality. The equipment produces an equipment-free (hyper-) reality-effect. One, indeed, fulfills the Woody Allen fantasy in "Purple Rose of Cairo" of living in a movie. Of course, the part one plays may be programmed by a corrections engineer.

Recline is into virtuality. The virtual torture chamber slides in behind visions of a perpetual Club Med vacation or an eternity in Las Vegas. This is where you will find the last man (interminably) hanging on. It is boring to see and hear the hype of hyper-space. After the 1960s, the counter-cultural neighborhoods became pornography zones. Probably the most popular family virtual-reality scenario will be visiting Disneyland in our VR suits. Anyone who thinks differently has not learned from Benjamin's unfounded optimism that technology would liberate. Recline does not mean that there will be any new contents. Just the reverse. One result of Crash is that there can be no new contents, just rearrangements of the old ones. Recline means taking everything that we already have into hyper-space so as to dwell in an environment saturated by "equipment" adjusted to produce a total imaginary that disguises it. Is being CAT-scanned much different?

Recline is expressed subjectively through the will to virtuality, that is, the will to be incorporated into technologically-produced environments. This expression signals the death of the future, of that which provided the excuse for the humanist formation and which continues as a resurrection-effect in the discourses of the priests (are the "pleasures of the text" ascetic?) of interminability. Recline gives up on the future: the future is the next virtual scenario. Benjamin again: "In 1932 Rudolf Arnheim saw 'the latest trend . . . in treating the actor as a stage prop chosen for its characteristics and . . . inserted at the proper place.'"[5] The will to virtuality is a will to be such a prop, to surrender to a scenario, perhaps as voyeur, perhaps as seduced, perhaps as sacrificial victim. Perhaps each by turns until, as E.M. Forster wrote, "The Machine Stops."

Recline is the great drift of the fin-de-millennium. But it is a horribly spasmodic drift, wrenched by bouts of retro-fascism erupting within it. The twentieth century has been festooned with "neo" movements (neo-Thomism, neo-Marxism, neo-liberalism, ad nauseam), all of which arise in the wake of the failure of nerve after World War I when the only political invention of the twentieth century, fascism, came on the scene. Anti-fascism beat a hasty retreat to the nineteenth century. "Ne(o)ver again!" We can no longer run after the future of a past that did not happen or that happened in an unforeseen and unsought way. All neo is now retro, even fascism, or better, is now *all* fascism, fascism here being defined as a nostalgia for a future, for self-vindication, for making good the losses in the "real world." In an age of recline, all idealism is fascism, an effort to make dreams come true when they have already been virtualized. Fascism as a cynical sign: "It wasn't supposed to happen again, but here it is happening again." Nothing is ever over. But, on the other hand, it is. Perhaps "ethnic cleansing" will allow "Hitler" to take a rest. The greatest TV event-scene of the '90s: the road north out of Kuwait into Iraq filled with a bombed-out traffic jam of vehicles of every description bearing pilfered consumer goods of every description. Here, the will to virtuality is bigger than retro-fascism. The hospice equipped with virtual-reality programs will be the preferred site of our death, not the death camp. A virtualized bad nursing home?

The Wish To Be Replaced

The will to virtuality is infected by the nostalgic belief, even as the behavioral organism seeks to become a prop, that technology is meant to serve the flesh. That belief is held cynically because it is obvious that the terms of the relationship were reversed long ago. The question must be raised as to why there should be any flesh at all (and, of course, the question has been often raised, mainly by VR hypesters—technology's Quislings and fifth-columnists). It makes perfect sense to conclude that if there are going to be total virtual environments, there should also be specially produced nervous systems to sense them. The deep wish of reclining (humanity?), after all, might be to be replaced. The bad conscience of the sense of interminability is the will to virtuality. The bad conscience of the will to virtuality is the wish to be replaced. The fin-de-millennium is the half-way house, the hospice, of a reclining species. Virtuality is what you do for/with/to (inferior) human nervous systems in the period during which custom-made nervous systems are being pre-pared and tested in human organisms. Benjamin again: "Hence, the performance of the actor is subjected to a series of optical tests."[6] VR-body as nervous-system testing. Humans as the best guinea pigs of all for the R&D of virtual intentionality. Animal rights anyone?

Post-Modem Theory: A Triptych

Anamorphosis: The Aesthetics of Virtual Reality

The will to virtuality is about the recline of Western civilization because it is the scene of a fatal acceleration: a virtual world where we finally achieve escape velocity beyond the gravitational pull of representational logic and break beyond the hysterical order of the ruling referents. A crash flareout where we enter the planetary space of anamorphosis, and in so doing experience for the first time the "non-space" of the third body, the third sex, the third skin. Anamorphosis, then, as the ruling aesthetic of virtual reality.

In the artistic practice of medieval times, the privileged aesthetic space was that of anamorphosis: the aesthetics, that is, of perspectival impossibility where the hint of the presence of a vanishing whole could only be captured by a glance at the reflecting surface of one of its designed fragments. A floating perspective where the part exists only to intimate the presence of a larger perspectival unity, and where the whole exists only as a momentary mirage captured for an instant by a spinning mirrored top.[7] Anamorphosis returns today as the privileged perspective of virtual reality: an aesthetic space never fully captured by its fractal fragments in its full seductiveness, and always dispersed and exaggerated by its mirrored counter-images. Just as the impossible space of anamorphosis can only be illuminated by the shiny surface of perfectly calibrated objects (spinning mirrors, musical instruments, sliver cones on glittering surfaces), so too are the outward signs of virtual reality found everywhere. Originating in the work of Flemish, French and Italian artists in the fifteenth and sixteenth century, anamorphosis has always been consigned to the shadowy and forbidden territory of the occult sciences. Because its refusal of the normalizing discourse of accelerated and deaccelerated perspective represented such a great rebellion against the representational optic of Western power, it was marginalized, passing into aesthetic remission.[8]

How could it could be otherwise? Anamorphosis was a genuinely outlaw perspective. Refusing the fixed aesthetic of foreground and background, and rejecting the reduction of art to a representational function, anamorphosis worked a more complex double game: a fantastic distortion of perspective, and the disappearance of representation into the non-space of illusion. This was an artistic gesture that functioned to destroy reality: transferring the ideology of fixed localized perspective into a seductive game of illusion. Anamorphosis is about the "perverted image."[9]

In the twilight days of the twentieth century, the occult science of anamorphosis returns as the seductive principle of distortion at the disappearing centre of virtual reality. Long consigned to the suppressed terrain of prohibited optics, anamorphosis now claims its place as *the* perpectival illusion central to the ruling technologies of digital reality. No longer is anamorphosis a perversion of power, but the aesthetic language of a power which perverts the representational logic of social reality. Anamorphosis is not simply a distortion of the real, but the disappearance of reality into a virtual world of technological automata and non-space. Like cynical reason and cynical power before, the illusional perspective of anamorphosis can return in a perfectly inverted form: *cynical anamorphosis* as the perverted image of virtual reality. There has never been a great difference between the spinning tops, glittering conical spaces, fantastically distorted cathedral murals of medieval times, and the automata of virtual reality today. What, after all, are VR suits, data gloves, and cyber-helmets but the fabulous automata of the aesthetic game of anamorphosis: a machinal assemblage that introduces the body to a fantastic galaxy of the perverted image?

In the visual world of anamorphosis there are no sight lines, no solitary (sovereign) subject as the privileged locus of accelerated and decelerated perspective, and no geometric grid for policing the perspectival simulacrum. What appears, instead, is a liquid world of fantastically distorted perspective: the space of illusion as non-space. Virtuality offers a third zone of liquid vision between distorted reality and its fractal distillate. It seduces us with the hint of our disappearance into the non-space of liquid vision that shadows its optical aesthetic of anamorphosis. Beyond the sovereign subject as the always fictitious locus of Renaissance perspective, to the non-space of the perverted image. This is what the technological imagination drives on, making our vanishing into the liquid inter-zone of the third eye so seductive. The third body, the non-space of the anamorphic nervous system: the dream world of virtualand.

The technologies of VR, therefore, are post-medieval surfaces where we merge with the aesthetic trompe l'oeil of anamorphosis, go liquid and become spinning tops, silver cones on glittering surfaces, a liquid array matrix. This is a way of breaking through to the non-space of the third body: that virtual space where the reality-function dissolves into a perverted image, and where reflecting surfaces are signs of that which never was. In the anamorphic space of virtual reality, we become the non-space of the perverted image.

The Illusion of Virtual Reality

There is intense fascination with virtual reality because it does not exist except as a sign of that which never was. We have never experienced the reality of virtuality, but most certainly have lived through the illusion of reality. A virtual reality that can be excessive in its claims because it comes under the heavy gravitational weight of the disappearance of the real. When reality is everywhere in refracted form, secreting itself into the tissue of the social like a mise-en-scène of its own vanishing, then we can finally discover virtual reality to be the space of fabulous illusion. Virtual reality, then, as a perspectival trick that virtualizes the real while working to actualize the virtual.

Anamorphosis is at the centre of the seduction of virtual reality environments because through it we are seduced by our own disappearance. Here, virtual reality is experienced as the actualization of art theory: the vanishing of the simulacrum into the non-space of anamorphosis. So then, an end to the debate on the death of the social with its fetishization of its object of critique—the simulacrum—and the beginning of the age of the *ambivalent* sign. No longer the death of the great referents, but their instant resuscitation in virtual form. Not the biblical legend of death and resurrection, but the virtualization of death—dead power—as the animating principle of the electronic skin. Consequently, an endless resuscitation of dead objects—dead fashions, dead sound, dead images—emerges as the energizing force of the technological galaxy: (cultural) retrieval and (digital) resequencing operate as the oscillating poles of ambient life in the electronic desert.

The will to virtuality privileges the ambivalent sign: frenzy and inertia, ecstasy and catastrophe, speed and slowness, crash and hyper-security, smart machines and stupid media. Never fused to a single polarity, the will to virtuality operates according to the logic of the double pulsar, simultaneously flashing contradictory sign-forms. That is its fatal fascination and its secret charm. The will to virtuality, therefore, acts as an *enfolded will:* always straining towards the most intensive expression possible of one singularity, while working secretly and immanently to undermine itself by the recuperation of the opposite sign-form. It is an enfolded will that plays the game of the doubled other: a cynical sign. Never more chilling in its reality-effects than when perfectly virtual, and never more historical than when already linked to the cybernetic logic of post-historical time, the will to virtuality disappears into violent crash event-scenes. We no longer live in the time of technology, but in the empty space of virtuality; not in the age of instrumental signification (technology as an efficient calculation of means), but in the great reverse arc of a dead power traced by crash virtuality. We are the first (electronic) inhabitants of the universe of pure symbolic media of exchange. We actually live out in the flesh the triumphant analysis of Talcott Parsons, America's Virgil. He describes the sociology of our quick cybernetic descent into a virtual reality as being marked by the (technological) revalorization of all the referents, from money and power to health and intelligence, as pure cybernetic processes. These referents are symbolic media of exchange that can inflate and compress, circulate and coagulate, because they occupy privileged spaces of homeostatic exchange in the great order of cybernetic being that is America Recombinant. In the days of the decline of the Roman Empire, only the Christians read Virgil's *Aeneid* with deadly fascination because they recognized in his diagnosis of the cause of the Roman decline (Christianity) a writing much to fear. Today only those marginal to American Empire still read Parsons for the same reason. Parsons' diagnosis of the vanishing of American empire into a virtual combinatorial is a chilling and apocalyptic vision of our own dispersion into the anamorphic space of virtual U.S.A..

The ruling illusions of virtual reality are everywhere. Consider the following event-scenes from the the empire of the virtual body and virtual politics.

Internet Flesh

Now that our electronic bodies have merged somewhere in the Spools and Slip gateways of the ethernet, we can finally get to know one another as electronic beings. Never fused to flesh but wired, never local but splayed across a global grid, not retrograde but immediate, and certainly never retrospective or durational but instantaneous. The virtual body knows itself only as white heat: a laser flaring out through the labryinthine layers of data in the net. Half-flesh/half-data, the electronic body is a pure virtual medium of exchange: a relational self that has meaning only as an empty quantum of information. McLuhan's "global village" with its promise of technology as a religious "epiphany" has passed. The cyber-net is now in *global gridlock*: a dense electronic matrix that, as Bruce Sterling writes, in *Islands in the Net*, mirrors back to us the human condition in all of its boredom and banality.

Xeroxing Bodies

Xerox's advanced research labs in Silicon Valley, California are determined to escape the stigma of paper: to mutate from copying paper to *copying bodies*. Their design for the electronic office of the future is guided by two key theoretical ideas: *ubiquitous computing and relational processing*. Ubiquitous computing refers to a radical transformation of the relationship of the body to the computer. No longer do single-user computers have a sovereign exchange-value for an informational economy. An organic "total computer environment" now vies for power in which the computer is driven by nano-technologies into infinite miniaturization: kitchen counters as computers, cups as computers, walls as computers. A telemetrically engineered environment in which the computer as the organic environment relates to the body as just another element in its sensory simulacrum. Here, the computer comes alive as a virtual medium of exchange with its own homeostatic drives towards "systems equilibrium." And relational processing? That involves the actual disappearance of the body into the computer matrix. No longer do single-user computers with a fixed, localized relationship dominate, but a Borg-like computer memory pool which processes all terminal-functions indiscriminately, effectively merges individual contributions to the solution of strategic corporate problems into a collective "bundle." Here, Parsons' theoretical analysis of the transformation of "intelligence" into mass cybernetic circuitry is graphically materialized. As the tour guide declared triumphantly: "Who needs a self anyway?"

At Xerox everyone wears "tab dogs," miniature computer sensors that relay telemetry to cyber sensors attached, like data surveillance cameras, to the ceilings of all the offices and hallways. And not just tab dogs, but "bird dogs" too for tracking all our "tele-friends": a computer screen across which are arrayed digitally composed images of all occupants of the Xerox lab. Here, we could see our cyber-friends drifting down hallways, congregating in offices, or maybe just loitering. As the Company likes to say: In the Xerox of the future, we finally understand that people really do not want privacy, and perhaps never did. Privacy is something that has been imposed on people by corporations. "We just want to do good for the human race," by providing technologies that allow us to mingle in the electronic flesh with our new best tele-friends.

And then I got it: Xerox has taken the concept of the electronic cuff worn by stay-at-home prisoners, and transformed it into the central principle of electronic office design for the twenty-first century. It intends to electronically cuff office workers (that's everyone), and copy their bodies into the cyber matrix. First their minds (relational processing), then their central nervous systems (ubiqitous computing), and finally their relationships (a tab dog for every worker, a bird dog for every bureaucratic complex). In contrast to the old panoptic ideology of Orwell's 1984 with its visible surveillance mechanisms, the seduction of the relational self is ingested to such a degree of intensity that the body delivers itself up for electronic execution. That is Xerox of the future: an electronic execution machine for harvesting all the bodily functions. The laboring body of the office worker is electronically liquidated, not in the name of punishment, but of a therapeutic version of freedom: the full cybernetic promise of actually "being networked," of becoming a telemetried node in the circular flows of the force-field of data.

The Xerox body, therefore, as a relational data base: a matrix of algorithmic functions, inflating and decompressing in response to changes in the electronic environment. Not the sovereign body, but the fully processed self that merges with the data envelope. Not the biological body, but the electronic body that finally comes alive as a flickering synapse in the galaxy of relational data bases. Not lungs trapped in an oxygen-dependency, but fibre optic sensors breathing in the static of the ethernet. And not skin, but liquid crystal arrays that shimmer and instantly reform with hologramic images of the body electronic. The Xeroxed body, then, is the emblematic fulfillment of Marx's "dead labor," just in time for the tearing down of the Berlin Wall and our fusion with the universal virtual (cybernetic) matrix.

Recombinant Art in the Age of Genetic Reproduction

No longer the work of art in the age of mechanical production, but now the work of recombinant art in the age of genetic reproduction.

Technology is art to such a degree of intensity that the world becomes a violent aesthetic experiment in redesigning the cultural DNA of the human species. A recombinant art that works in the language of biological engineering: cloning, transcribing and resequencing the genetic code of the human species. *Cloning* refers to the genetic reproduction of the human species as model replicants: some all a (radio) ear, others with a (televisual) eye, a privileged few with a (surgically altered) face, some speaking with a (floating, algorithmic) tongue. The privileged elite emerge from an iconic gene pool (Madonna from a cultural gene pool for transgression and games of post-seduction; Liz Taylor from a media retrobase for the "feminine beauty myth").

Transcription refers to the sign slide at the disappearing centre of recombinant culture. A floating informational economy where cultural genotypes are sampled and retranscribed at random. In the universal media archive image sampling is the rule and cancellation to the degree-zero is the overriding (genetic) imperative. Scenes of exterminism camps appear simultaneously with those of NBA basketball games. Reports from Texas execution chambers alternate with sunshine weather reports. In the technological archive, technologies of communication do not so much merge (fax, cellular telephones, computers, VCRs, TVs) as they are genetically transcribed within a universal media combinatorial. Here we find fax computers (modems), telephone TVs (the digitally enhanced electronic highway), and cellular VCRs (new "routing" technologies). Japanese consumer electronics manufacturers have transcribed a boating practice into a marketing strategy—bringing onto the market in quick succession an overwhelming number of incrementally improved consumer electronic products to prevent competitors from entering the market with a single consumer product line. The practice of "boating" electronic products is better known in the industry as *churning*. In the electronic body archive organs are transcribed at will: space-age plastics become aortic valves, baboon hearts beat in the human chest, and dead fetal tissue from Russian abortion clinics becomes source material for recombinant genetics in California research universities. Integrated media, integrated species, integrated imaging, integrated (electronic) personalities: a cyber-culture of "monstrous hybrids" emerges.

For *resequencing* think of contemporary trends in fashion where there can be a cultural recuperation of the retrograde because we have already passed through to the space of virtual culture: a processed culture that codes its past like a vast archival data base (clothing styles, smells, looks), resequencing the present as a way of disturbing the stasis of the field. Retro-fashion, then, is comparable to a Slip Gateway in the electronic net where the cultural trends of yesteryear can be randomly retrieved, instantly respooled, globally distributed in electronic (media) marketing envelopes, and then sprayed like a fashion-ethernet on selected population targets in promotional culture. Consequently, the swift emergence of the culturally hip look for the "huppies" (the sixties yippie sensibility combined with the eighties yuppie money) of the nineties. Now the dress-down of "grunge" travels across the force-field of Nirvana, and the dress-up spandex hippie now becomes corporate tie-dyes, designer bell bottoms.

The Fashion File is the privileged site of virtual culture. Here, culture disappears into endless virtual resequencing: a perfect reciprocity among universal media elites who retrieve sign-fetishes from the archived past as ways of energizing a fading present. Marketing agencies lurk around the consumer net scoping new trends by means of digitally wired focus groups. Advertisers quick-process the sounds and images of virtual intentionalities, and the electronic body (that's us) desperately needs to be distracted from the implosion of the post-Christian self. The Fashion File, therefore, as the cultural equivalent of computer "phracking." Like elite hackers, fashion creates noise in the void of the electronic body. Breaking into the virtual cultural archive, it retrieves new looks as electronic counter-measures, transgresses the (metaphoric) social field with metonymic cuts, disturbances, and incisions, and creates monstrous hybrids as a way of stimulating a cultural system that always threatens to collapse into an inertially grounded field.

Technology as recombinant art in the age of genetic reproduction marks a great evolutionary shift in human history. No longer are genetic history (biological) or social history (simulational) separate and distinct, but simulation and genetics are now conflated under the sign of the *virtual gene*. Such is bio-technical reality where technology as the will to virtuality comes alive, and assumes a species-existence of its own: the *virtual species*.

And so, the question: What are the characteristics of bio-technical reality, of a living virtual reality? The answer might begin as follows. It originates with the merger of genetics and simulation where blood turns into electricity. Living virtual reality has a combinatorial logic and an anamorphic aesthetic. Its language comprises digital codes and the electronic frontier is the hyper-space within which it functions. Cellular walls form the electronic network, worms and data infections are diseases that are treated with cyber-therapeutics (data vaccines). A living virtual reality functions in the time of recombinant culture, whose sociology is based on splicing, cloning and sequencing. Its economy is organized according to the ideology of pan-capitalism. And its fatal destiny is to recline into the age of the weak will. Post-modem theory begins with living virtual reality as the cybernetic form that postmodern history takes in the age of Lenin in Ruins (Post-Marxism) and the West in Ruins (Post-Liberalism). Post-God(s), then, for the time of the "conscience-vivisections" (Nietzsche) and body vivisectionists (Marx).

What Are We Waiting For?

The vanishing body has been resuscitated, just short of vacuity, as the circulating body. The body has become a circulating medium of exchange, coursing through the mediascape: my sadistic home video for your confession that you're a transvestite priest. The wired body is also the scanned body—input and output—a fully colonized alpha and omega of, by, and for the mediascape. The "biological" (scanned and wired) body is an image resource for the mediascape and, for the time being, its image actualizer.

The fin-de-millennium is defined by the inadequacy of the "biological" organism, that is, perception, to the anamorphosis of virtual reality. At one and the same time virtuality is the only credible alternative—the body feels itself to be inferior to the body image, the mediascape is positive and all the rest (why call it "world"?) is privative— and virtuality is unbelievable because it has not totalized itself. Here is the ground of the will to powerlessness: a constitutive sense of inferiority to the mediascape, an inability to achieve it because it is "only" anamorphosis. The perverted image (perverted as image exchange-value) and the ambivalent sign (fanatical and cynical) are the effects of the dependence of the mediascape on "biological" bodies as image resources and image actualizers. The wish to be replaced is partly an effect of the body's consitutive inferiority to an anamorphic perceptual field.

Lynne Cohen, a Canadian photographer who shoots the interiors of organizations, revealing the bizarre scenes that grow up in the garden of reason, shows us what we are waiting for to replace us. In "Laboratory" we look into a room with two empty chairs flanking a nude mannequin which is cut off at the waist and inserted into the top of an electrical apparatus (the apparatus replaces the sex organs: electronic machine sex). Two audio speakers face the mannequin. Here is a prototype of an image actualizer, a being that can truly appreciate the refinements of an advanced sound system.

Our replacements will be severed at the waist and plugged into virtual reality. For them anamorphosis will be total. They will surely be poor image resources but they will have at their disposal the Fashion File and the wonders of recombinant imaging. They will be engineered for eternal recurrence.

Our replacements will be vastly superior to ourselves as image actualizers: they will be built for anamorphosis. Welcome to the post-God era.

Meditations on Post-God

Does the will exist? Or are we beyond Nietzsche's "will to power"? Are we living in the reverse spiral of the "will to powerlessness"? What sickness results? Who could tolerate the will that consumes itself? Who could stand up to the arc of a dead power? With the death of Marxism, we have finally come to the end of Christianity. Post-Christians and Post-Marxists, then, are perfect equivalencies for the Age of Lenin in Ruins which mirrors the Age of Reagan in Ruins.

The grisly age of the post-Christians appears as faded images of the *Book of Revelation* on the one hand, and a desire for conspiracy theory, as the only possibility for narrative closure, on the other. A diseased time of weakness disguised by authoritative (but visibly risible) cultural overrides: smut TV, blip consciousness, techno-fetishism, true confessions as lies most of all.

Post-Christians are the sickliness that ensues from the will to powerlessness. We know that Christianity "solved" the crisis of divided experience by the Augustinian act of the "will to will": that is, to subordinate the body to the confessionality of the saeculum. Here, the triadic coordinates of experience—will, intelligence, emotion—finally

Lynne Cohen
Laboratory

fuse in the perfect exterminism of the will to believe. What happens when the trinitarian formulation crashes, just disappears, and we are left with the historical horizon of classicism: Retro-gnosticism?

Can we still speak of the intensification of the nihilism central to the will in terms of the "will to will" (Heidegger)? Or should we speak of the sub-will, the will that wills its own abandonment? Is the will to virtuality about shedding life, strip-mining intentionality until only aimlessness results? Drifting would be the consequence: an aimless culture that yaws before the black sun of its own exterminism. Vanishing into the event-horizon of the electronic network where only positionality matters: Are you "upstream" or "downstream" of the binary controls of data flows? What happens when the body vomits, splits apart, becoming a brilliant array of floating organs without a body? Deleuze's "the body without organs" could describe an earlier (Catholic) moment of cultural encryption that could be resisted by an enhanced positivity, but the epoch of "organs without a body" is closing time: bodily organs drift away, then reappear as pure cybernetic code. The seduction to be code versus the dead-hand code of the body of flesh and blood.

The body spasms: the screenal economy of electronic pleasures invades the previously darkened regions of bodily organs, illuminates their deficiency, and substitutes a virtual network of organs without a body. Electronic organs for the body digitalized: a migratory path of designer organs for quick exits from the history of the flesh: virtual eyes, virtual tongues, virtual touch.

The Post-Christian body spasms: it never could tolerate the unbearable tension of divided experience, so it slides into virtual intentionalities for a virtual reality. It plugs all the bodily orificies of everyone with technological circuit-breakers. Seeing is watching TV, hearing is MTV, sniffing is coke, feeling is Deanna Troy, thinking is wetware. Split consciousness for a split culture: a veneer of predatory public behavior over an inner reality of soft parasitism. A long-vacated self that reinforces its armature for quick excursions across the public domain by spraying its social construct with narcotics. In an interview on 20/20 a male college student states: "I only have fun when I'm drunk...I'm more relaxed, more sociable. I like myself better." A female college student on the same show concurs: "When I'm drunk it's the only time I don't think about what I look like, about my lipstick . . . I even forget to go to the bathroom." But the post-Christian body is also cynically sentimental: Cher travels to

Armenia dressed to the teeth in the very niftiest of Malibu Armenian chic. She gets two episodes on 20/20 to display her Hollywood charity: "Why, if the mother of this child could get the letter, this little piece of paper, about her sick daughter to me all the way in Malibu, I'm going to bring this girl back to America, to Malibu." Barbara Walters can only shake her head and say: "Cher is fabulous. She does it all for altruism. And you know I asked her: 'Twenty years ago when you were Sonny and Cher would you have done this?' She told me: 'No, then I just wouldn't have cared.'"

The Post-Christian body spasms: words float in seas of vomit, smiling eyes chill-down for the kill, lips peel away into culture grinders, heads shriek that they are melting down into a "thousand points of light." But still it's fun: the Post-Christian body loves the games of the cynical sign, admires the transparency of the double meanings as the electronic body confesses and confesses. Adorno once said that the highest form of cynicism is to see right through the manipulation of advertising, yet still buy the product. He was still a modernist: now only virtual products under the reign of the cynical sign are interesting. The Post-Christian body loves itself *because* it wants to get rid of itself, to deliver itself up to its virtual shadow. In Virtual America you can only be truly intimate if you tell your darkest secret before a TV audience of millions. The private self of the post-Christian body is too haunted by its own secrets, too busy building up the walls of the crumbling cultural superego to tolerate the strain of private confession. But then it smiles at the petty conveniences and takes its place in the new class structure of virtual reality described perfectly by the spatial architecture of jumbo jets: comfort class, business class, and first class.

More Meditations on Post-God

A piece of Nietzschian wisdom: In order to break tables of value you have to violate conscience. When life is strong and ascending it is a boon to violate conscience, because every transgression feeds the will to power. The reverse is true for declining life: every transgression saps the will to power.

When life is ascending, smashed tables of value are immediately replaced by new ones as though the new tables of value were organs of life growing from within. The old tables of value become a mask of dead skin that as it crumbles reveals a new and living face with the ripeness of late youth. All is plenitude: not a moment of vacancy between old and new, no "interregnum," no waiting.

So different from Nietzsche's characterization of nihilism in *The Use and Abuse of History* where he imagines life reduced to a mask with nothing behind it: the Fashion File, endlessly circulating through the anamorphic landscape—the body as a mobile mannequin, now xeroxed, that is, existing *to be imaged*, in standing reserve to be challenged forth to be a resource for the virtualized mediascape. All of this has already happened. There was nothing new to replace them when God's tables of value were smashed. Life had been so corrupted from the inside by the virus of the "soul" that it could not bring forth new tables of value. In a state of recline there is no will to power. The old tables of value have been smashed but guilt remains and along with it regret, nostalgia, and resentment—all the reactive dispositions and emotions. Everything goes retro, to provide the content to be reflected and reproduced anamorphically. Guilt is so wearing that life no longer wants to *feel*. In a massive value inversion—the extremity of *ressentiment*—life convinces itself that it is more real and true to be digitized than to breathe. Life is no longer just a waiting game in the hospice, a diversion until the replacements go on-line; but a resource base to be turned into data base and then to be recombined (interminably?) as the circulating body (image) coursing through the networks. So, "human beings" have already been replaced. They have not simply vanished. They are currently resources for imaging—not for imaging *technology* (technology is a hot tool), but for the process of *imaging* that replaces the life-process. Not so much the vanishing body, though the androids will be here some time, but the body for recombinant imaging, a resource base that is kept ready for service by being perpetually dosed with images so that it identifies with them and craves to be among them, to BE there itself, to be saved. Not just the body for fashion, though that too, but the body as a fashion that sometimes goes out of fashion. Why is it that you can only be truly intimate and tell your darkest secret before a TV audience of millions? Because "you" as flesh and feeling are no longer real. By being televised your biological body is rendered inferior to the image of it, the *ens realissimum*. You are thereby temporarily relieved of guilt because now your double is bearing it. You are the resource base for your televisual double. Complete remission of sins can only come through the ultimate paradise-sacrifice—always being on TV, perpetually challenged forth by the mediascape, the most welcome interpellation of all for reclining life. Reclining life is prey to the guilt-effects of an impotent conscience that no longer supports any tables of values but that can continue to punish transgressions of codes that no longer summon belief. Virtualization is also, maybe more than anything else, relief from the punishments of a conscience acting in the name of dead values, the direct effect of dead power.

CHAPTER FOUR

The Political Economy of Virtual Reality

Data Trash analyses the political economy of virtual reality by advancing seven key theorisations concerning the overall structural logic, political implications, and (post-) historical dynamics of virtual reality.

1. Pan-Capitalism

There are neither ideological nor institutional alternatives to capitalism for the first time in history; no resistances to check it, no independent criticism of it to keep it honest and on its toes. Capitalism is on its own and must confront alone its homicidal double: fascism. Capitalism, here, is not a model of production or consumption, but something very different: Nintendo capitalism. Virtual capitalism for the age of wired culture, where exchange-value disappears into the recombinant commodity-form and where money itself vanishes into the circulatory relays of the high-speed backbone of the Net. Pan-Capitalism is the myth of capitalism in its final sacrificial phase, strutted out for one last burst of circulatory violence of exchange before it too is consumed by wired culture.

2. Surplus Bodies

Pan-Capitalism is typified by random outbursts of sacrificial violence directed against those rendered surplus to the political economy of virtual reality. With the eclipse of communism and the seeming sovereignty of virtual capitalism and, with it, of the recombinant commodity-form, the traditional political space of contestation between Left and Right disappears, providing a privileged opening to the ascendancy of new (telematic) forms of fascist politics. Everywhere in the age of pan-capitalism, fascism is resurgent. No longer fascism in its original European form (nostalgia for the lost sign), but its reinvention under the recombinant sign of pan-capitalism as virtual fascism: a set of political symptoms of the hatred of existence, the will to will, the will to virtuality, the (death) wish to be replaced. Virtual fascism is a social movement in the sense of Talcott Parsons: membership in the societal community is based on particularistic criteria and takes priority over every other disposition toward existence. Therefore, virtual fascism is defined through a quest for purification of the societal community, which is a reaction formation to the self-defilement of the hatred of existence. Virtual fascism not only reacts against self-defilement with purity, but also projects the hatred of existence as a will to abuse those who are signified as external to the societal community. Politically and economically fascism is stochastic. As Ortega y Gasset pointed out definitively from a study of a normal, even bland, fascist, Primo de Rivera, fascism "lives from hand to mouth," is always campaigning against something, and favors direct action over discussion and negotiation; that is, it is void of both policy and process, a political vacuum filled by the leadership principle and by coercive discipline. Virtual fascist economics is a null category, congeries of irrational nostrums and sacrificial disciplines administered to the societal community—adventures in self-annihilation. Virtual fascist politics deals in the sacrificial coinage of surplus flesh: bodies that are rendered surplus to the continued functioning of technotopia, and thus made available for one last role as sacrificial victims for the media-net.

3. Abuse Value
The primary category of the political economy of virtual reality is abuse value. Things are valued for the injury that can be done to them or that they can do. Abuse value is the certain outcome of the politics of suicidal nihilism. The transformation, that is, of the weak and the powerless into objects with one last value: to provide pleasure to the privileged beneficiaries of the will to purity in their sacrificial bleeding, sometimes actual (Branch Davidians) and sometimes specular (Bosnia).

4. Virtual Capitalism
The structural dynamism of the will to virtuality. Virtual capitalism is the constitution of telematic networks of imaging and signifying that

outerize and invade the behavioral organism, and use it as a resource base and sensorium for creating a techno-mediascape that will function without (human) behavioral organisms. Virtual capitalism disciplines and recruits bodies through the mechanisms of profit and debt, both of which have been virtualized and function as politico-ideological signs rather than as descriptors. Virtual capitalism is based on total circulation through the telematic networks, through which everything is virtually exchangeable. Virtual capitalism is perpetually failing behavioral organisms, placing them in a state of insecure dependency. When virtual capitalism creates insecurity through its perpetual displacements, (recombinant) fascism comes in to mobilize the hatred for existence.

5. Virtual Politics

The state is constituted by the disciplinization of that which resists virtualization. The root dynamic of virtual political economy, its crux, is the opposition between the hyper-liquidity of free circulation (virtual capitalism) and the stasis of behavioral organisms (societal community). The state mediates this opposition through a virtualization of compromise formations. The two political regimes emerging under pan-capitalism are liberal- and retro-fascism.

6. Liberal Fascism

The liberal state, which mediates virtual capitalism to the societal community and the societal community to virtual capitalism via the constructs of neo-conservative/neo-liberal ideologies becomes an agent of punitive disciplinization to refractory bodies. Through the bunker state liberal fascism excludes surplus bodies (immigration), through the austerity state it uses debt reduction and high unemployment to control labor and minimize social programs, and through the security state it submits bodies to testing and surveillance. Under liberal fascist ideology everything done to victims is for their own good or is regrettable action that is necessarily performed for an obvious over-riding human(itarian) interest. The dominant mood of liberal fascism is cynical piety; its strategy is positionless power—the continual displacement and circulation of policy initiatives mask the failure of mediation and the inability of political institutions to cope with the liquid speed of virtual capitalism. Liberal fascism lacks a strong presence of certain features of fascism proper, particularly the feature of direct action, although it resorts to the latter (going after Koresh, Aidid, Noriega) whenever its own procedures are wanting. Serving virtual capitalism and a contingent societal community, liberal fascism is a compromise formation between the technological liberalism of prosperous times and the retro-fascism of times of degradation.

7. Retro-Fascism

The fascism proper that was never supposed to happen again returns with a vengeance, creating the bi-modern situation of hyper-technology and primitivism. From one viewpoint, socio-biological-linguistic organisms (human beings) mediate virtuality to each other and themselves. That is the instrumentalist view of virtuality. It's German Chancellor Kohl deciding not to use TV to save himself from embarrassment over neo-Nazi violence. It is just standard modern social science (humanism). From the other perspective, virtuality mediates human beings to constitute itself. How is that possible? The will to virtuality and the wish to be replaced are the human dynamos that energize virtuality, its material causes. An alienation of the "human" through the flesh is required to put virtuality into being. The socio-biological-linguistic organism makes itself available as a resource base for imaging technology and assorted body invasions.

Within the context of the double mediation, fascism is determined as the reaction formation against the logic of virtuality—the life of waiting to be replaced under the sign of the wish to be replaced. Fascism rebels against recline, against the "last man," proclaiming: "We can do it. Causing suffering will do it for us." And is the following cynicism or vicious innocence or just the truth? "Yes, we'eve seen it all before and we like what we've seen." What could be more fun than some death camps? The masochism of liberal (fasc)ism, administering virtuality in the name of safety, is matched by the sadism of retro-fascism. What could be more fun than some death camps?

Pan-Capitalism

At the same time that virtuality proliferates and the flesh becomes a resource base for the mediascape the material conditions of virtuality implode. How long can this condition last before there is a crash? The imagination aggrandizes as the environment and infra-structure degrade: the revenge of matter. The economy degrades, politics degrades, the societal community degrades . . . the mediascape (culture) aggrandizes.

These are the material conditions that result: Over-indebtedness ("debt-liquidation cycle" common in depressions), resultant trade wars. And something new emerges: pan-capitalism without any alternative but its homicidal double—fascism. Capitalism must fend off fascism without the help of socialism, which is dead economically, politically, socially (the proletariat?), and as a signifier. That is the political-economic conflict of our time, intersected at every point by the processes of virtualization. Virtual fascism? Pan-capitalism as the mechanism of virtualization (capitalism parasites the will [to be replaced]), encounters its homicidal double.

Pan-capitalism hits in the midst of a classical depression: a debt liquidation cycle. Why there is "over"-indebtedness is not a question for political economy, but for the kind of existential psycho-ontology that identifies a general state of recline and an attendant will to virtuality. For an existential psycho-ontology with its inspiration in Nietzsche-Heidegger-Baudrillard, the contraction of destabilizing debt signals a profound loss of confidence in the flesh. Despoil the future generations. Hate the future. Hate your progeny. There is no future for them, only a *virtual* future.

The will to virtuality gets an economic boost from a depressed economy. Virtual satisfactions are cheaper. Movies do well in depressions. There is a TV in every hospital room. Can we doubt that it will not be long before every hospital room comes equipped with a virtual reality helmet? A cyber-punk "fantasy": You check into the hospital. As soon as you hit the bed the helmet goes on and it doesn't come off until you're released except for when it's time for you to go under anaesthesia.

Virtual satisfactions are cheaper. This is how the hatred of existence works. A nihilistic will, projected against future generations, motivates indebtedness. Under the sign of possessive individualism possessed individuals work the economic destruction of the future in the name of just deserts, security, and self-fulfillment. "Who cares? I'll be dead before the shit hits the fan." "Are we having fun yet?" Smile buttons. Smile signs on canisters of pesticide in the chemical fields of the great midwest.

Do not blame the situation on narcissism. That is what liberal communitarians like Alasdair MacIntyre and Christopher Lasch do. Narcissism is a reaction formation against the nihilistic will to destroy the future (for the flesh). Communitarians expect a synergistic effect from a managed gregariousness of reclining bodies. But what is the synergistic effect of reclining bodies in one of those hospitals with virtual-reality helmets?

Hyper-indebtedness indicates a massive case of viciously acquired naivete (Josiah Royce). Liberal apologists will dispose of the above by saying that we've made an effect into a cause; that is, just because the effect of hyper-indebtedness is the spoliation of the future doesn't mean that a will to spoliate the future causes hyper-indebtedness. While this argument is logically impeccable it implies that we're supposed to accept ideology as the explanation of conduct. The "culture of narcissism" begs to be explained by something other than its own appearance, the current garb of that old devil, selfishness, the master-name of capitalist psychology. Why, it's simple. Who wouldn't want a BMW and a box of Godiva Chocolates? The neo-cons think it's just human nature to want these things. The neo-libs think it's just corrupted human nature to want these things, and that they can rectify us through (the joys of) "service." We say that only a nihilistic will can be so viciously naive.

A nihilistic will spoliates the economic future. As that future becomes present, virtuality becomes the preferred means to manage and canalize demand, which in turn incites the flip side of nihilism—the will to virtuality. In the bi-modern condition, nihilistic hatred and nihilistic recline alternate in a dialectic of spasm and crash, each betokening hatred of existence.

The above discussion of indebtedness does not cancel the thesis that the debt is virtual, a mirage manipulated by the state apparatus to discipline and deny populations. The debt functions simultaneously on the levels of realist and virtual political economy, depending upon the chains of signification in which it is figured.

Here is how virtual capitalism works: NKK, a Japanese steel company with a failing shipyard, converts the shipyard into a facility to produce simulated domed beaches, complete with wave-making machines and surfing contests. The selling point is that nothing unpleasant, uncomfortable, or inconvenient happens at these beaches: the last man's paradise. Virtualization in the name of exchange value is the formula for the transition from industrial capitalism to virtual capitalism.

What is capitalism? Here it is simply the valuation of labor according to its exchange value and the valuation of consumption according to purchasing power; that is, a Marx-inspired view of capitalism. The peculiarity of capitalism, for Marx early and late, is the fetishism of the commodity—a genuine step into virtualization. Embodied labor becomes a calculable factor of production and the embodied consumer becomes a sales figure. Kick away the nostalgic notion of alienation and you are left with labor as productivity and consumer as purchaser. All in the name of getting more out of a sale than you put into it. Virtuality arrives through the efforts of profit-making enterprises to find new markets when they are under stress. Virtuality sells.

The essence of capitalism is to be whatever effective demand makes it. In a money economy (a capitalist economy oriented by exchange value) purchasing power determines production. Producers attempt to induce and seduce demand through the virtualizations of advertising and promotions, but it is an overstatement to claim that they create it. Rather than the Frankfurt School's viewpoint that the masses have been addled by repressive desublimation, we suggest that virtuality sells to a nihilistic will— a last man who goes to the virtual beach. All in all, the higher cost of admission to the virtual beach is more than made up for by reduced transportation costs and time saved in transit. But is that why people go to a virtual beach?

Virtual capitalism: a world-wide profit-making system struggles mightily to serve a nihilistic will, of which it is an expression—exchange value is already dead and infinitely mobile. Purchasing power rules in capitalism. Capitalism is the way by which purchasing power comes to prominence in the constitution of the human's productive and consumptive relation to the world. Purchasing power demands virtuality and capitalism is always already virtual.

Pan-capitalism is the great dare that the last man can be satisfied, that bodies can be placated sufficiently to make the transition from the flesh to its replacement, that the hospice can be made comfortable and secure. Meanwhile surplus flesh accumulates.

Purchasing power contracts in a depression. There is not enough to go around and there's no fat cat to bail you out. Technotopia starts crashing.

Virtualization is applied by the structures in dominance, but the flesh also must confront itself in the vulnerability of recline. Depression means the possibility of being economically lost. The flesh rebels, but the flesh is in recline. The result is the austerity state.

The state, under current conditions of pan-capitalism, functions to administer austerity to a population that has been conditioned in hi-tech consumer economies to desire a virtual paradise. The frustrated will to (happy) virtuality turns into the terror of economic abandonment: the nightmare of "homelessness." As Deena Weinstein notes, the homeless are not wired. To contrast, think of the legion who are kicked into the production machine and then kicked back into their holes where they are wired and re-charged for another day's production of virtuality. Austerity is the public policy of managed depression. The people do not like it. Maybe they will not take it from a (post-) liberal state. Fascism— getting ours expressly at the expense of others—is a live option. Austerity in itself is a form of injurious neglect.

Austerity is sacrificial capitalism. The state, in the name of protecting the flesh in the herd-form of an ersatz "nation," carries out planned sacrifices in order to wring out the debt. "Who benefits" is replaced by "who suffers." Only the wringing out takes forever. A managed depression might turn out to be interminable, a permanent depression. "Don't move too fast; you'll pull the economy into recession." Why not reflate the economy? Who's afraid of fascism? Getting used to less is the economic fate of reclining life.

Reclining life still has enough will to power to rebel against economic insecurity, but not enough to affirm itself as flesh. Choose your nihilism: virtualization or the (self-) infliction of harm. They also go together well. In Freud's sense, the death wish takes a circuitous route to its destination: in this case—half-and-halfer last men punish (themselves) in the name of security, but not to the point that they get out of needing to keep punishing. The austerity state is a compromise formation made for those who simultaneously will to live and will to die, but whose will to die, to virtualize, has at last become clearly dominant over its opposite. But is not the austerity state a recognition of the importance of future generations who should not have to be paying off debt forever? That too, as it kills and virtualizes. The austerity state is a loaded compromise formation.

Virtual Economy

Virtual economy is seductive because it "grows" wired culture like a wildly mutating cancerous tumor: a crash-site that moves from the world of highly differentiated cellular (economic) organization to an undifferentiated (tele-)organic mass. Having no energy of its own, the tumor economy feeds parasitically off the flesh and blood of the host organism. A body invader of reclining flesh, the tumorous mass of the virtualized economy is a perfect parasite/predator, depending for its very existence on the standing-reserve of old flesh and blood, but always willing itself to become *the* sovereign life-principle. Fascinating because always fatal, the virtualized economy is the vanishing-point for the disappearance of the now superseded order of capitalism into the will to technology.

And why not? Virtualized economy is an economy of disappearances: the disappearance of the main factors of capitalist production (labor and products most of all), and the disappearance of the key *relations* of production (the class system of classical capitalism). No longer an *economy* any longer, it represents the vanishing of the economic into a global virtual space of telematic transactions. The wired economy quickly dissolves products into relational processes, labor into networks of cybernetic knowledge, and consumer "purchasing power" into *political* opportunities for policing interventions by the austerity state through consumption taxes. In the age of virtuality only the speed of circulation matters. A nomadic economy that is already post-economic: where capitalism is preserved as a mise-en-scène distracting the eye from the liquidation of the real material relations of production, and the triumph of the virtualized commodity-form.

No longer the age of commodity-fetishism (capitalism in the modern age) or even of promotional culture (capitalism under the sign of postmodern pastiche), but now the *recombinant* commodity-form. In virtual capitalism, the recombinant commodity functions like a hard-wired digital sequencer, cutting and splicing the surplus matter of the wired economy into electronic bytes: imaging bytes, sound bytes, body bytes, smell bytes, and money bytes. Here, the (organic) body spasms as it vomits into the desert-like void of the electronic body; TV mutates into a complex cybernetic system patching the body electronic into the neural networks of liquid capital. The old world of manufacturing is forced to move at strobe light shutter-speed as it is resequenced across the time zones of hardware, software, and wetware. Flesh itself becomes a welcoming orifice for penetration by all the molecular ganglia of the digital economy. Like a circuit diagram for the hyper-charged Pentium microchip, the recombinant commodity is always positionless, endlessly circulating and fully relational: an invisible (post-economic) architecture that is imposed on the grid of the electronic body. Never capable of being comprehended in its discrete elements (there are none), the recombinant commodity-form is a violent force-field, a screenal economy whose dynamic logic is digital reality, and whose destiny involves the disappearance of really existent material conditions into the vanishing-point of the will to virtuality.

The recombinant commodity has no (earthly) home, only an electronic sim/porium. A rootless nomad, it wanders restlessly through the liquid circuitry of wired culture. Renouncing its interest in property-relations, it yields fealty only to the empire of speed: the new polity of pure process (economy). Abandoning the tired dialectic of use-value and exchange-value, the recombinant commodity finally discloses itself as a fatal doubling of abuse value: process-abuse for the organic body, and a fatal register of the coming abuse of the standing-reserve of surplus flesh, surplus labor, surplus populations, and surplus states. The recombinant commodity must abandon use-value because the rest position of the referential signifier is death. It must renounce the (alienated) pleasures of exchange-value because recombinant culture occupies the mirrored world of recursive space. Refusing both the alienation of the laboring body in capitalist market exchange and the reification of the fungible body in the promotional phase of the high-intensity market setting, the recombinant commodity works the (fibre optic) vein of the ecstasy of disappearance.

Politically fascistic, culturally a cynic, relationally a sociopath, and psychologically an exponent of object-relations theory, the recombinant commodity is the operating system at the (algorithmic) centre of virtual economy. All the rest is a (computer) *application*: TV channels as abstract vectors of data entry-points into the electronic body; designer fashion as digitally coded applications of technology outreach by promotional culture; model body types (the "waif look" so fashionably cachet in the 1990s) as bionic constructs straight off the shelf of wired culture; and sudden audience mood shifts as psychological registers of the channeled flows of the media sensorium.

As the operating system of virtual economy, the recombinant commodity functions as a *circulating medium of virtual exchange*. Think of Marx's (virtual) theory of the fetishism of the commodity-form in (re)combination with Talcott Parsons' perceptive, but as yet theoretically unappreciated, analysis of a full-fledged cybernetic system (Virtual America as the world hologram) consisting of dynamic homeostatic exchanges among "symbolic media of exchange." Here, the organic body vanishes into its electronic Other as the recombinant commodity works to impose a virtual system of *moral economy* as the new world cybernetic grid. Driven by the dynamic language of the will to virtuality, the cybernetic grid has as its underlying logic the enhancement of (its own) adaptive capacity by the continual redefinition and resequencing of virtual (value) patterns. Virtual debt, virtual populations, virtual labor, virtual money, virtual resources, and virtual wars result. The conquest anew of the disappearing zone of the organic is processed through the violent circulatory system of virtual exchange. Certainly not static, the medium of virtual exchange undergoes accelerated phases of radical expansion and contraction. Its *expansionary* phase comprises the will to virtuality; and its *deflationary* phase is marked by neo-fascist forms of direct action. Neither purely virtual nor essentially fascistic, the circulating medium of virtual exchange *is both, and simultaneously so*. The will to virtuality is typified by the over-authorization of cybernetic logic (the moral value-principle of virtual economy), and by the delegitimation of economic "resourcing." At its extreme, this results in a virtual credibility crisis: a crisis of confidence on the part of virtualized populations in the ability of the technological class "to deliver the goods" (the debt liquidation crisis as purchasing power contracts and consumption taxes interpellate the consumer body). The fascistic turn of virtual exchange is marked by recurrent patterns of direct action interventions in the world situation (from the officially authorized murders of the Branch Davidians in Waco, Texas, to the bombing of the Iraqi "spy headquarters" and suburbs while Clinton attends Sunday church services). These patterns are a certain sign of the disappearance of power from the empire of virtual reality. Taken to its extreme, the contraction of virtual exchange towards fascist direct action threatens to dissolve the recursive logic of *cybernetic primitivism* towards its most fundamentalist code-elements. Technotopia crashes: burnout is signalled by the brilliant luminosity of final flareouts of a reclining empire.

The High-Speed Backbone

The virtual economy is a bio-economy, a living species come to life at that point where capitalism has been eaten by technology.

If bio-engineering can be an object of such fascination (nano-technology, retinal screening for heads-up body scanners, recombinant genetics) it is because it is a mise-en-scène, presenting in the form of a futuristic fiction what has already happened to us as we were fast-sequenced through a processed world. Consequently, the steady announcement of new telematic "discoveries"—such as, molecular computer chips, cell-sized *nano* bio-engines for "invisible travel" through the blood stream, new genetic hybrids from the labs of all the recombinant geneticists—attracts not a ripple of discontent nor a muted cry of ideological discord because these manifestations of "technology outreach" into the body electronic are less a brave new horizon of telematic wilderness clear-cutting, than an already nostalgic sign of our (wired) past. In virtual economy, we have always lived through a specious present of nano-subjectivity. The disappearing body fast dissolves into relational networks. Retinal scans objectify the scanning procedure that the imaging-systems of the electronic body have long demanded as their fateful dispensation. Molecular computers, travelling in the blood stream, are late-comers to a post-human scene where the recombinant body has long ago been uprooted from its earthly ground, and compelled to re-enter the sea of floating data. Ours is that curious age of *future-nostalgia*, where the screenal economy of the electronic body registers in advance the spreading shock waves of the will to technology. The much-hyped culture of new wetware at the body/ machine interface, then, constitutes object-displacements of a massive (telematic) reconfiguration that is always already post-history to the post-human body. A high-speed backbone, the virtual economy is always on over-drive as a spinal tap grid for the matrix of virtualized flesh.

The speed of *immediacy* is the prevailing logic of virtual economy. Always moving on fast forward, the recombinant commodity smashes national barriers, drains off the surplus energies of local economies, and resequences regional trading zones (EC, NAFTA) until they synch with the strategic objectives of transnational capitalism. Following a vector that approaches the speed of light, the ideological rhetoric of the recombinant commodity is always the same: virtual *boosterism* (techno-logical euphoria) mixed with a dash of technological determinism (virtual *necessitarianism*).

In the wake of the violent passage of the recombinant commodity, social detritus remains. Post-(human) bodies surface for quick electronic assimilation into the neural network of virtualized exchange. A post-(jobs) economy typifies a virtual technology that works to disappear the working class. A post-(immigrant) culture dominates technological societies that garrison the fading benefits of social security in the bunker state. And a post-(leisure) culture awaits a virtual time when nothing is more active than the electronic body that, like Brownian motion, is maintained in a constant state of turbulence. The high-speed backbone of the recombinant commodity, therefore, anticipates the age of post-capitalism. A perspectival trompe l'oeil, capitalism can now exist only as a vanishing-point whose dynamic energy masks the disappear-ance of the product-economy, and the triumphant emergence of process-economy.

Alt.Bondage..Alt.Sex..Alt.Fetishes: On Growing a Cyber-Body

Simply switch on your Mac/Dos screen, and the ideology of virtualized capitalism is brilliantly displayed. Everything is there. Bodily flesh is reduced to a digital servomechanism. The centering-point of organic perspective is displaced outside normal ocular vision to the nowhere space of virtual optics in the Net. Individual subjectivity crashes as it swiftly merges with an info-economy of data bytes. Here, the mind is filtered by organs without a body, and the body is suspended in the illusion that digital reality maximizes the zone of freedom (misplaced [virtual] facticity), *whereas actually we are (finally) growing a cyber-body*. Those flickering screens of personal computer "work stations," therefore, as fantastic sites of embedded flesh for virtual capitalism. The personal computer functions as performance art for the body electronic, a densely encrypted ideogram as virtualized flesh zooms across digitalized space. Switch on the power, and the electronic grid is immediately activated (RUA-CYBERSPACE); switch off the energy and the force-field of the cyclotron instantly falls into high-voltage inertial ruins. Crash and inertia, (global) immediacy and (territorialized) localness, hyperspace and bounded time: this is the mirrored world of the endlessly recursive virtual flesh.

Indeed, what if "Windows" were not a computer application, but a form of elevated (telematic) consciousness? In this case, we could speak of the sequencing of the body electronic as a switching-station: a multi-platform site for downloading and uplinking data. Hard-wired to the speed-backbone of the universal BBS and addicted to a diet of fibre-optics, the "Windowed" body would become that which it always thought it was only using: a file-transfer function. Bodies with plugged-in, high-performance editing studios for cutting, pasting, and copying the mutating scenes of the imaging system. "Windowing" memories for filing the event-scenes of post-history in the matrix of quick-access folder flesh. Utility-functions for re-energizing the recline of the body with organs with new android menus: *Adobe Illustrator* speech, *Pagemaker* writing, *Micro-Mind Director* for re-editing visual reality, and *Real-Time Digital Darkroom* for a substitute sleep-function. *Double click...delete...It's now safe to switch off your machine*: the slip-stream rhetoric of the android processor.

Forget philosophy: all the super-charged debates among nominalism, sensationalism, analytical positivism, and critical theory have been abruptly displaced by the emergence of MS-DOS as the ruling epistemology of virtual reality. *Virtual positivism* for the era of windowed culture: a recursive space of ambivalent signs that slips away into an infinity of mirrored, fractalized elements. Not only a gateway culture, but a Windowed process economy as the terminus ad quem of virtualized capital, occupying no fixed geographical space, but colonizing the imaginary landscape of digital dreams. A screenal economy put into the command-function by an elite of sysops manipulating the language of internal disk drives, but containing nonetheless an indeterminate array of file menus: a perfect act of homeostatic exchange between code-functions and emergent value-principles. Certainly not a closed cybernetic universe of input-output functions as envisioned in positivist sociology, but an imploding universe at the violent edge of an impossible refraction between opposing tendencies towards crash and systematicity.

Crash is the open secret of virtualized economy, and on behalf of which capitalism mutates into the will to technology and the latter into the will to virtuality. Capitalism in its windowed phase *demands* the crash experience: scenes of primitive energy where the fibre optic backbone of the system as a whole is strengthened by the sudden reversals at the vanishing-centre of crash. Crash capitalism is the desired-object haunting the imagination of virtualized flesh. In that impossible reversal between primitive direct action and windowed data exchanges, between abuse value and virtualized exchange, is to be found the driving momentum of virtual economy as disappearance. When we can speak of money as suddenly hyper-driven and flipped into virtual, twenty-four hour data exchanges, of the slip-streaming of consciousness, of feeling as software to the hardware of the electronic brain, and of spooled politics, then we can also finally know virtual economy as a fatal, delirious crash-event. The organic body shatters into mirrored fractals, vision explodes into a delirium of virtual optics, speech dissolves into the ecstasy of the rhetoric machine, and the sex organs happily opt for the alt. bondage file of future sex.

In the windowed world, we pass time by slipping into our electronic bodies, deleting for a while the body with (terminal) organs, and becoming *alt. subjectivity* in the ether-net of organs without a body. The drag of planetary time eases, and we flip into the hyper-role of "lurkers" wandering through the virtual rooms of the city on the digital hill. Voyeurs of our own disappearance into a recombinant subject-position: perfectly relational and positionless, and, for this reason, fascinated all the more. All twitching fingers as we become a computer keyboard, all burning sex as we stand around the dark edges of virtual bondage dungeons, all drifting feelings as we slip from node to node on the electronic net, and all virtual intelligence as we actually dissolve into a mouse that cursors across hyperspace.

Our technological future has never been more transparent: *alt.bondage, alt.sex, alt.fetishes, alt.conspiracy, alt.TV Simpsons, alt.nano-technology, alt.politics, alt.Star Trek, alt.Bosnia, alt. jokes, alt. vacant beach...*

The Virtual Class

The *universal* interests of the recombinant commodity are carried forward by the *particular* interests of the technological class. Itself a virtual class because its historical interests are linked to hyperspace and its economic relations are (globally) coextensive with the world network of technocratic elites rather than bounded in local space, the technological class fuses with the high-speed backbone of the Net. Its expression as the emergent class of post-history is coterminous with the sovereignty of the recombinant commodity.

Having no *social* origins, the technological class is a bionic product of that vast, and demonstrably successful, experiment in *economic eugenics* that has been unleashed by the merger of technology and biology in the post-historical form of the will to virtuality. A mutant class born at that instant when technology acquired organicity and became a living species, the technological class is itself a product of combinatorial logic. It stands as the first, self-conscious class expression of the universal net of post-human bodies. Alternatively therapeutic in its cultural outlook, because it believes fervently in technology as coeval with the life principle itself, and vicious in its defense of the political interests of the will to virtuality, this class uniformly, globally, and at the same historical moment flees the closed boundaries of the nation-state, going over to the side of a new eschatology: the interfacing of cybernetics and flesh as the (post)-human good. In its bitter struggle to break free of the fetters of local politics and to differentiate its universal (virtual) interests from the particular interests of the disappearing working class and inertial public sector bureaucracies, the technological class must mobilize on behalf of the ontological claims of the will to virtuality. Consequently, its *political* aim: the virtualization of economic space with the abandonment of products, and the sovereignty of process economy. Its *territorial* ambitions: to colonize hyperspace as voyagers exploring the stellar regions of the electronic frontier. Its really existent *community*: co-relational and co-extensive networks of cyberneticized knowledge. And its prevailing *ideology*: an ambivalent, but no less enthusiastic, doubled rhetoric of technological fetishism and technological determinism.

Not a passive class, but aggressive and predatory, the technological class has an immanently global strategy for its swift coronation as the leading class of post-capitalism. The Virtual Manifesto, with its associated war strategy, proceeds as follows.

1. *Tactical Envelopment:*

On a global basis, the logic of tactical envelopment functions by installing supra-national trading blocs (EC, NAFTA, the newly emergent South-East Asia Economic Co-Prosperity Zone). This function consists of a political strategy for undermining state sovereignty and freeing up the speed of virtual economy from the gravitational pressure of local regulatory "circuit-breakers." These circuit-breakers include local state subsidies for particular class interests in the production economy, environmental standards, tariff barriers to the unfettered movement of the process economy, and nationalist coalitions mobilized around social agendas of labor and its representative political parties. Here, suborned technocratic state elites work hand in hand with the virtual class to ensure, by law and trade agreements, the unhampered movement and statutory protection of "intellectual property" (relational networks of cybernetic knowledge) through the permeable walls of local political space.[1]

2. *The Disappearing* State:

Under cover of the GATT negotiations, with their ideological recuperation of the obsolete dogma of "free trade" (itself a mise-en-scène for the disappearance of merchandise capitalism), a struggle is waged to destroy the internal integrity of the interventionist state and to free up labor as a fully mobile, fungible and, hence, virtualizable commodity.[2] Here, the liberal-democratic compromise of the "welfare state" is swiftly and decisively pushed aside in the interests of the virtualization of economic space. The state that cannot plan in the interests of its own social economy and that cannot act on behalf of its own political economy is also the disappearing state. It is a perfect subordination, therefore, of the manufacturing phase of capitalism before the transnational interests of process economy, of (local) property before relational knowledge, and of bounded political sovereignty before the primogeniture of the recombinant commodity.

3. *A Definition of the Virtual Situation:*

Resequence the ruling rhetoric of particular political communities according to the global ideology of technological liberalism: that political consensus which holds that the dynamic and unimpeded expansion of the will to virtuality is the *superordinate aim and justificatory condition* for the state policy-making apparatus. Witness the evangelical appeals for a "high-speed digital superhighway" across the United States as both the aim of a technologically renewed America and its ethical raison d'être (for a technocratic U.S.A. "capable of competing on an even playing-field with the rest of the world"). Construction of a new high-tech transportation infrastructure (the famous "Chunnel," the modelling of the "new Europe" on the super-quick network of the French TVA) mimics the construction of the Canadian National Railway across the Canadian frontier as a vaunted act of "nation-building" (long before Western Europe was "Canadianized" by technological liberalism). The downloading of Tokyo, floating airport and all, into a virtual cyberspace, complete with neon libidos and pulsing video screens on every (telematic) street corner. In each of the above cases, it is a different country, but the very same ideology of technological liberalism. The will to virtuality is both the aim and justificatory condition for the territorial expansion of the space of the political (state).

4. Ideological Delegitimation:

Finally, through concerted public policies that speak the language of technological necessitarianism, struggle to delegitimate unions and their political defense of the working class. Under the onslaught of techno-cratic elites occupying the heights of right-wing governments across the OECD, union leadership and their working class membership are con-tinuously ridiculed as nostalgic defenders of an already superseded economic order. The unemployed are also targeted for abuse. In Canada, federal and provincial governments enact socially sadistic policies to-wards the jobless and the homeless because, from the moral viewpoint of the technological class, these are fully surplus bodies, accidental spillover from a virtual system that must result in growing social inequalities and the creation of a permanent underclass. With its inherently religious commitment to virtualization, the technological class would find it irrational, and thus immoral, to speak to social issues that are endemic to production. As in Cronenberg's *Dead Ringers*, the bodies of the technological class may look normal on the outside, but on the inside something has gone terribly wrong. They are mutants: half-flesh/half-wired, fetishists in virtual guise who work to liquidate, by absentee mindlessness, the working class, the homeless, and the powerless. And, of course, if "benign neglect" does not work, then there is always recourse to the deterrence-violence of the security state. In the United States, employment in security forces is a growth industry.

As David Cook states in a reflection on Thurow, Galbraith and Reich as emblematic signs of the recline of the American mind:

> With the satisfaction of desire (contentment) comes the growth of the military and the private security industry. The controlling mood is one of violence and force. . . In America there are no longer, if there ever were, "Good Americans", or "Toquevillean citizens", or the "fortunate" who are going to look into the future. America is in the process of disappearing, dispersed across the world in a continuing sacrificial spiral. America now as reengineering itself via technological processes that create the culture, work, competition and self that is no longer "made in America" or made anywhere other than in technological space and whose future may well be played out in the only realm that America still holds the edge—violence both inside and outside the nation.[3]

Virtual Class War

The technological (virtual) class must liquidate the working class. It does so through alliances forged with political representatives of the global technocratic class. The working class is grounded in localized space; the technocratic class wills itself to float away in the virtual zone of hyperspace. The working class has an objective interest in maintaining steady-state employment in the production machine of capitalism; the technological class has a subjective interest in transcending the rhetoric of employment to "creative participation" in virtual reality as an ascendant life-form. The working class depends for its very existence on shielding itself from the turbulence of the nomadic vector of the recombinant commodity by securing its political foundations in the sovereignty of the nation-state; the technological class, politically loyal only to the virtual state, thrives on the violent passage of the recombinant commodity. The working class, grounded in social economy, demands the sustenance of the "social welfare net"; the technological class flees the inertial drag of taxes on its disposable income by projecting itself onto the virtual matrix.

Deeply antagonistic and with immanently warring interests, the working and technological classes are the emblematic historical signs of the beginning and the ending of the twentieth century. The modern century might have begun with the great historical struggles of the working class, sometimes revolutionary (Marxist-Leninism) and sometimes reformist (the welfare state with its trade and business unionism), but it certainly ends with the political victory of the technological class, and with the global retreat of the working class, like a tide running out to the postmodern sea. Lenin and Capitalism in ruins are the mirrored signs of the disappearing working class, and the triumphant ascendancy of the technological class as the post-historical embodiment of the will to virtuality. Consequently, the collective gloating of the technological class and the diffusion everywhere of virtual reality as the implacable horizon that welcomes us to the twenty-first century.

What of the relationship of the technological and capitalist classes? They are not the same, since the capitalist class has an interest in an old *value-form* of production (surplus-value), and the technological class has its interest in a new *relation* of process economy (virtualized exchange). The capitalist class seeks to ride the whirlwind of virtual economy via quick translations of process into products (consumer electronics); the technological class parasites surplus-value as a way of actualizing the virtualized body. The capitalist class desperately seeks new digital technologies as investment strategies for conquering the mediascape, and with it, all the welcoming orifices of the electronic body; the technological class puts its research at the behest of capital accumulation, while it awaits the inevitable vanishing of capitalism into the will to virtuality. Refusing in the end to accede to its own historical liquidation at the hands of (an already obsolescent) fealty to the production machine, the capitalist class goes over to the side of the processed world of virtual economy. It puts capitalism in the service of the will to technology. In return for providing the material conditions necessary for allowing the machines to speak and to have (cybernetic) sex, the virtual world responds by rewarding this new class of virtual capitalists beyond its most feverish dreams: the robber barons of primitive capitalism are replaced at the end of the century by the pinhead egos of software barons. Capital is virtualized. Property remains in place and workers are sequestered, but resources are virtualized and redistributed from the virtual population to the elite. But, of course, capital has always been virtualized, always a matter of transforming material reality into a floating world of surplus-exchange. This process of alchemical transmogification of nature and social nature finds its most abstract, and essential, expression in virtual reality. Virtual economy is a way of finally coming home for the liquid, circulating rhythms of the recombinant commodity.

Consequently, our actual situation is this: the state remains behind to sequester those who cannot, or will not, achieve escape velocity into hyperspace—wage-earning workers, salaried employees, broad sectors of the old middle class. The political model here is simply, "If in doubt, tax," because the Carceral State energizes its fading energies by randomly selecting among the virtualized population objects of abuse value. And the territorially imprisoned virtual population responds in kind: it initiates a form of popular counter-terrorism by transferring all political leaders into liquid targets for the pleasures of abuse. Abuse and counter-abuse, then, as the doubled codes of territorially bounded space and its sequestered virtual population.

As for the technocrats? They have long ago blasted off into hyperspace, filled with sad, but no less ecstatic, dreams of a telematic history that will never be theirs to code. An evangelical class, schooled in the combinatorial logic of virtual reality and motivated by missionary consciousness, the technological class is already descending into the spiralling depths of the sub-human. It wills itself to be the will to virtuality. In return for this act of monumental hubris, it will be ejected as surplus matter by the gods of virtuality, once its servofunction has been digitally reproduced. In Dante's new version of the circling rings of virtual reality, this class operates under the sign of an ancient curse: it is wrong, just because it is so right. For not understanding virtual hubris, it is condemned to eternal repetition of the same data byte.

Slaved-Functions: The Political Economy of Virtual Colonialism

Virtualized capitalism is about cynical power, not profitability. Here, the virtual order of capitalist exchange is a global grid for the terminal division of the world into the shifting order of sadism. The truth-sayer of virtual capitalism as power is to be found in those dispossessed countries and regions that are fully surplus to the telematic requirements of the will to technology. Residual spaces outside the operating system of the recombinant commodity, the surplus-economies scattered around the globe are preserved as sites of pleasureful abuse value and as potential sources of surplus flesh, doubled scenes of what might happen to us if we fail the will to virtuality. If the electronic body is neither a privileged citizen of the dialectic of technology (the spiralling network of programmer/consumers across the neural network of hardware, software, and wetware economies), nor a cursor in a clonal economy (the "five tigers") for quick simulations of the telematic order, then it can only be a "slaved-function": a detrital site of surplus body parts for the fatigued organic bodies of the "master-functions" as they await processing into virtualized nervous systems. Master-functions, slaved-functions, and clonal economies, therefore, as the classificatory power grid of virtualized capitalism.

Consider, for example, India, Haiti, Bangladesh or the continent of Africa. These countries have slaved-economies that are maintained as standing reserve for the "master-functions" of the ruling sim/porium of Japan, Western Europe, and North America. Not really part of a global welfare system administered by the UN/US, but surplus nations that are sites of novel experiments in body vivisectioning and vampirism in its late capitalist phase. A whole underground global trade, then, in body parts (livers, hearts, blood) that are surgically cut out of the surplus flesh of the virtualized population of slaved-nations. And how could it be otherwise? The organic body knows that it will die before it can be morphed into a virtualized state, and so it desperately scans slaved-bodies, particularly those of the young, for the elixir of life: kidneys, pancreas, eyes, and hearts. And why not scenes of mass innoculation as first-cut film scripts for the future of the body electronic? That's the mass injection of the AIDS virus into the blood streams of Africans, before an officially approved and hyper-charged AIDS virus under the cover of a "hepatitis vaccine,"could be downloaded into the bodies of gay men in New York and San Francisco. Slaved-nations also function as marketing sites for the chronic diseases expelled from the aestheticized culture of North America: the aggressive promotion of cigarettes to the citizens of slaved-nations, under the always seductive sign of the "Marlboro economy," provides symbolic, if not actual, membership in the master android cultures. Or, for that matter, why not copy the discarded cultural kitsch of America (Disney World) to the modernist cultures of Western and Eastern Europe as symbols of their clonal status in the lead societies of virtualized capitalism? No longer, then, the division of political economy into first and third worlds, but a more grisly dissolution of the virtualized globe into a sadistic table of sacrificial value: *master-functions, clones, and slave-functions.* When capitalism disappears into a power grid, then economy remains only as an illusional space, disguising the more sadistic ruse of technology as abuse value.

Virtual colonialism is the end game of post-capitalism. Just when we thought that the age of European colonialism had finally come to an end, suddenly we are copied into the second age of virtual colonialism: a reinvigorated recolonization of planetary reality that reduces human and non-human matter to a spreading wake of a cosmic dust-trail in the deepest space of the blazing comet of virtual capitalism. A recolonization of everything is in progress, including the virtualization of labor as jobs in the productive sector are downloaded around the globe to a slaved work-force; the virtualization of culture, as the planetary noosphere, from Canada to Romania and China, is caught up in the deep-space drift-net of CNN and MTV, which beam out the pulsar code of America to the clonal cultures of the world. The virtualization of fashion is also part of the body program as, for example, designers resequence the (recombinant) color and style of clothing into a high-fashion Internet. "Soft fashion" produces surplus-virtualized exchange (for itself) by transforming the culture of fashion into a digital sequencer, linking child labor in slaved-nations with the high-intensity market setting in the master triad (Japan, Europe, and America). And virtualized transportation, too, as transnational automobile producers flip into process economy: robotizing production by copying and pasting parts manufacturing to pools of cheap labor, while maintaining virtualized populations as holding pens for (ad) stimulated desire.

If there could be such a fantastic display of publicity about 1992 as five hundred years after the conquest of (aboriginal) America by Europeans, it is probably because 1993 was Year One of the reconquest of the world by virtual capitalism.

Sacrificial Violence and the Technological Class

Fascism is the politics of the transition from the flesh to virtuality. It has been going on at least since St. Augustine's fabrication of the Trinity and perhaps since St. Paul's fabrication of Grace, the former creating a dead power called "spirit" and the latter alienating the body from its proper means of salvation: self-cultivation. Yet these two inventions led to the most horrid self-inquisitions and lacerations of the flesh in the name of delivering itself to its savior. Today the savior is virtuality, what the Trinity and Grace were made of to begin with.

The flesh has (been) failed. The signs of this fact are the operations of the will to virtuality (from the simple taste for simulation indicative of declining life to the sacrificial adventures in virtuality of the death wish) and the re-appearance of fascism (the greatest of all nostalgia movements)—life driven by hatred (of itself) to destroy the other (and then itself). Life that has too much will to live to suicide directly, but not enough to stop the suicide from taking place by a circuitous route. Fascism: the losers revolt. The flesh is losing. There's a crash. The flesh turns on itself. Take your choice: the VR helmet or the the disciplinary state. There are two options for failed flesh, both of them nihilistic. At the present historical moment both are appearing in extreme form, shaping the structure of the bi-modern. Fascism is the (fatal?) spasm in the transition from the flesh to virtuality (that is, from the flesh to crash—when the whole media-net falls apart). The choice is butchery now or crash later (perpetually). The media-net falls apart: all the hardware, software, and wetware crash, but, no worry, the bodies have already disappeared. Or, alternatively, the will to be replaced is successful and the androids take over the media-net and make it work for them some way or other. Cyber-torture anyone?

Virtual Torture

The national evening news presents a pure case of virtual torture. When the French police arrest someone for not buckling up their seat belt when they are driving, the poor culprit has a choice of paying a $50 fine or taking a ride in a torture machine that simulates what it feels like when your car rolls over. It looks like an amusement park ride, but it's meant to scare you straight. For your own good. Is it any wonder that France produced Foucault? Virtual disciplinization.

Recombinant Fascism and the Virtual Class Resumed

Recombinant fascism is a twisted, tortuous, brutal way to the self-annihilation of a flesh that cannot tolerate its own existence in the light of its deficit, its loss. There is no better example in the contemporary world—indeed, this is a textbook case of classical fascism revenant—than Greater Serbian Nationalism, issuing from the loss of Serbian power in the territory of former Yugoslavia. It becomes a matter of *protecting* Serbian populations by transforming them into predator-parasites. Fascism always needs to punish. Revanchism. Homicide as the last station before suicide. An (essential) operational definition of fascism: People with severe self-hatred attempt to save themselves at the expense of others and receive secondary sadistic gains from exacting the expense. That is fascist economy (*social* economy) (moral economy): the installation of abuse value as an operating principle. Recombinant fascism makes abuse value the memory core of the political economy of virtual reality: fascism finally sheds its nostalgia for the lost sign, making of the will to purity an empty, and consequently all the more delirious, resurrection-effect.

Recombinant fascism is the politics of (stateless) capitalism and (state) communism in Ruins. Pan-capitalism has no politics of its own: virtual capitalism obliterates politics in a liquid flow of lightening quick transactions and substitutions. Ever mutating numbers in data bases—pure screenality--are its elements. There are no politics without bodies. In recombinant fascism bodies turn upon each other and themselves in sacrificial orgies of surplus flesh. All in the name of belongingness with other bodies that are supposed to be distinguished in some special way as an all-embracing social entity, what Parsons called "the societal community," a "nation." The individual (Reagan) and the class (Lenin) are dead as political formulae. The nation is very much "alive" as a pure resurrection-effect running on empty. We are privy to the Nietzschian herd in a state of panic paranoia. Recombinant fascism is the limitation of capitalism by a flesh at war with itself. It can also be (virtual) capitalism's agent of body disposal. The nation is adventitious. Weak life is always herdlike. Recombinant fascism: an epiphany of resimulated sign-values—nationalism/racism/sexism/humanism/super-humanism. Those are some components of the contemporary adventitious conjunction that makes for the (always) virtual "societal community." Recombinant fascism is the fetishism of the societal community as an aggressive reaction formation against a death wish. Hence its appeal to purity—a form of death in life. And all this in the name of "community" because each needs the others to confirm the self-deception of heroism, superiority, and goodness. All in the name of some bodies at the expense of others. Fascism—making flesh expendable: hyper-capitalism. Sacrifice.

Virtual Politics

> The economy is growing and American companies are prospering but the announcements of job cuts this year are more numerous than ever. . . Job shedding has become fashionable—the mark of a good manager.
>
> New York Times, March 22, 1994

Pan-capitalism is in a perpetual state of crash. With no social norms to limit its "instrumental activism" (the Parsonian term for the "spirit of capitalism") it spirals into a liquid frenzy of the accumulation of symbolic media of exchange (Lenin's "finance capitalism"). From there it spins into the cyber-space (which capitalism's productive apparatus generates) that annuls it. Capitalism's incessant seduction of purchasing power is trumped by the will to virtuality, which meets it on the other side of labor.

Pan-capitalism is ceaseless displacement of anything that is not instantaneously mobile. The futures-index trade relayed from Tokyo to Chicago to Dakar within seconds is its Platonic paradigm. Labor is the antithesis of the capitalist ideal of liquidity. Labor cannot be moved that quickly. The flesh remains inconveniently rooted to the earth, though "man" aspires to soar through the galaxies. Pan-capitalism is endlessly recombinant. Left to itself it works to realize itself as a mutating relational data base. The flesh as labor and purchaser suffers injurious neglect in the transformation of product into process, the recombinant commodity.

The recombinant commodity is not even sign value. It is a packet or "body" of information transmitted to determine the operations of computer systems linked to other computer systems in networks of instantaneous exchange and substitution: telematic capitalism.

Labor is dying and with it the flesh. Telematic capitalism speeds the automation of production, shifts the sites of production with amazing rapidity, and panders to the will to virtuality, all of which creates a pile-up of surplus flesh. In addition it retains the characteristic of classical capitalism of recurrent financial crises (over-indebtedness-debt-liquidation cycle), leading to recurrent depressions: injurious ne-glect of labor. At the same time capitalism is not yet fully telematic and still has need for some labor and some fleshly purchasers. Enter fascism, which mediates between dying labor, itself constituted by the opposition of the will to live and the will to virtuality, and the abstract accumulative will of capitalism, itself an intermediate form of the will to virtuality.

Not all of those animals that belong to the human biological species fit into the liberal idea of "Man," always an ideal in the vicious sense. Some of those animals are excluded altogether and most of those animals are excluded most of the time. It can get so extreme that the liberal (Kant) speaks for a "rational being" that he admits does not exist in an enfleshed form. Then to make matters worse he gloats about his opinion that you can never know whether or not you have performed a moral action unless you experience the suffering of a surrender of desire in order to perform the act. Liberalism reveals itself as sadistic and sacrificial. Liberalism is constituted by injurious neglect of the thing.

Is it fair to make Kant stand for liberalism? The greatest good for the greatest number. The legitimacy of regulating other-regarding action. The generalized other. The supremacy of the legal state. Liberalism is always sacrificial and communitarian. But liberalism is dead. It has been absorbed into the rhetoric machine as a second-order simulacrum. Liberalism has its true contemporary home in the hospice of "medical ethics" where liberals debate the sacred issues of who should be given livers and hearts for transplantation and in what order. Liberalism under the sign of ether.

Liberalism's cultural place was long ago taken by the operative ideology of what was called "liberal democracy": technological humanism. Tech-nological humanism is the notion that "humanity" can remake the world through technology into a garden of inconceivable delights for the species being. Marx and Dewey, the twin stars of technological human-ism, said it all: the unity of theory and practice. Heidegger saw it and proclaimed it: technological humanism crashed in the death camps.

Post-crash, the will to virtuality has taken over. Technology becomes an environment to which organisms adapt or (and) die. It does not belong to them. It serves most the will to virtuality. Fascism becomes the operative political formula, mediating the tendencies of the classes constituting virtualizing society. The dominant political system of post-liberalism is virtualizing fascism, that is, liberal fascism—the growth of fascism as a tumor under an exhausted skin of liberal rhetoric. It faces another system, retro-fascism, the anti-matter of virtuality: kill it all before it virtualizes.

Take a look at technotopia for a moment. Each organism will have its own VR generator, which will be on all the time. Each organism will be able to choose whatever event-scene it wants to be in, whatever scenario it wants to participate in (gender, even sex, might be selected at whim). Not to worry about solipsism. Organisms might share event-scenes (virtually, of course): they would interact with each other through cyber-space, each responding to the other who would be virtually present in each one's scene. Each would dwell in private fantasy at whim. This is as total a freedom as the Eurocentric mind can imagine for finite flesh. In technotopia the possible finally gains complete supremacy over the actual, through virtuality.

Definitional note: Virtual reality, virtuality—The generation of a space for events within the organism's perceptual space that substitutes for that perceptual space, dominating the organism's perception with the event-scenes that occur within it. The preceding is virtuality as fully realized, actualized. Virtuality can also be used in another way to include partial or imperfect perceptual substitutions, such as that rendered to visual space by such visual media as painting, photography, cinema, and TV, all of which generate spaces that supplant perceptual space. The will to virtuality is the will to supplant the organism's perceptual space with a virtual space and thereby to supplant social time with heterogeneous virtual temporalities. Technotopia is the perfection of liberalism. Each one is its own God. Or perhaps this is the advent of the Leibnizian monad activated in its virtual armor by fulgurations from the media-net. Technotopia is the death of liberalism. It is virtual solipsism. It has always already crashed before it would ever come to be. It is the dream of a species in a hospice waiting interminably to be replaced. But it is a dream that keeps materializing in the most grotesque ways.

Try Oceania. It's a habitat being promoted by a group in Las Vegas that is to be built on the ocean (outside the hurricane zone) where inhabitants will be out of reach of the state and bureaucracy and will be able to live according to the vision of Friedrich Hayek and other great individualist-capitalist-libertarians. A step on the way to technotopia.

Technotopia crashes. An HIV Prison Camp for Haitian boat people at Guatanamo is a lurid example. What about an intensive-care unit? The flesh cannot sustain virtuality. It still has to interact with its own kind to get the basic necessities like food. It still cares about "the world" and its place in it. Yet it also wants more than anything to be virtualized. Out of this contradiction between a debilitated Eros and virtualized Thanatos grows liberal fascism.

Make the world safe for virtuality. That is the principle of virtual liberalism. Of course, not safe for the complete riot of possibility that the technotopians have in mind, but for what the media conglomerates program. The virtual liberal state exists to keep those with purchasing power wired to the mediascape and those without it under control (human-rights discipline in Somalia). It protects the media environments of suburban homes from threats from the world underclasses. It accommodates retro-fascist movements (the Christian right in the U.S.A.) and safety fetishists (eliminate violence on TV, test everyone for drugs, etc.), but its mediation is whenever possible in favor of the right to virtuality, that is, virtualization on the terms of the mediascape.

The virtual liberal state retains the individual-rights rhetoric of liberalism, but it is not a rights-based system (as though there ever was one). It functions to defend a fictitious societal community in order to virtualize its members. If only there was perfect prosperity. Then the virtual liberal state wouldn't even seem to be regressive to those who lived within it. But when economic contraction hits, more and more organisms are excluded from the ability to enjoy recline. The state shows its basis in sacrificial violence as it disciplines and punishes.

Liberalism must mediate the virtual class, which uses states as mere conveniences, just as it uses corporations, to prepare the way for the replacement of *homo sapiens*, all in the name of technotopia; the capitalist class, which uses the virtual class for accumulation; and the vanishing working class, which degenerates into purchasers of virtuality and surplus flesh. In times of general prosperity the tensions within the class structure are resolved in favor of ever-more virtualization of the population. The contradictions appear when capitalism and virtuality fail, and the state must impose austerity.

The virtual class will never risk its own skin. That's why so many of its members support Ross Perot. The typical virtualizer cannot exist outside an organization—a virtual environment. The virtualizer is fetishizing its own flesh. It wants to end up in a hospice, forever. Who thinks up viciously naive and bubble-headed fantasies like Oceania and an existence in which each one gets to choose their own reality? The real VR types are power trippers out to do mind-reaming, all in the name of absolute individualism. Who sets up the cyber-space, anyway? This is the technical component of the virtual class. The other component is the organizers—entrepreneurs who bring the media-net to be and work its transactions: the virtual commodifiers. They exist between and take over the organizations in which the technical virtualizers nest. Take Perot. He parasites the government, sells it software, creates an army of technical-organizational virtualizers. Suckling from the organization to preserve the dear flesh while you make the flesh disappear. Virtualizers are the agents of recline, the greatest recliners of all. They produce, sell, and impose recline.

But there is more to Perot. After parasiting the government he turns against it in the name of the people. He claims not to be expressing his own preferences, but to incarnate the American people's will. He taunts the legislature. He takes direct action through the mediascape. He's a retro-fascist *and* a virtualizer—a figure embodying all of the contradictions in virtual political economy.

Perot produces one of the great recombinant commodities of all: data-processing services. He has translated his flesh to the mediascape: his body-image can populate it almost at will. He doesn't care where he makes his money. He's a virtual fascist. He also leads a national renovation movement in the name of a mythical societal community based on collective (shared) sacrifice. A flesh-saving movement at the expense of others (American economic supremacy). He's a retro-fascist.

The contradiction in Perot is the contradiction in virtual political economy. One hand renders the flesh superfluous and the other leads the flesh in a revolt against its superfluity, but always cynically, transacted through the mediascape...until and unless it turns to carnage. Virtualization or carnage. That is the present horizon of political possibilities.

Where does capitalism fit? Capitalist and technocratic elites play both sides of the street. Sure they would prefer the interminable speed of virtualization to death camps. But they will take death camps. They are instruments of the fluctuations of the flesh as it virtualizes and rebels, moves back and forth between "liberal" and retro fascism: the politics of the bi-modern. The bi-modern reveals its structure in times of economic austerity when recline becomes uncomfortable. Liberal-retro fascism is irritable recline.

CHAPTER FIVE

Prime Time Reports

MICHAEL JORDAN MOGADISHU

The NBA championship game between the Phoenix Suns and the Chicago Bulls is flickering on the screen. It's half-time, and the news announcer suddenly appears to say that the game will be interrupted for a military news burst from the skies over Mogadishu, Somalia. It was the Persian Gulf video all over again: greenish night vision, shadowy C-131 attack planes fading away in the darkness, brilliant phosphorescent explosions of the bombs as they blew away the headquarters of Aidid, a Somalian clan leader. I was prepared for this: the mediascape had signalled my electronic body for days that this was an "uncooperative" clan leader who needed to be punished (he was held responsible by the UN for giving orders to attack the Pakastani contingent). I also knew that after Clinton's passivity on Bosnia, and his shrinking away from Lani Guinier, that the President needed a quick military kill, particularly one that could be done at a safe telematic distance without the direct involvement of American ground troops.

Curiously, as this screenal display of pure war flipped back to the NBA game, the sports announcer said: "And now for the always awkward transition back to basketball." But, of course, this was the true confession which was a lie. My electronic body felt only a deep symmetry between the war scene in Mogadishu and the virtual war on the basketball court in Phoenix. Maybe there was not the slightest disjunction between these two screenal economies because we witnessed two coeval wars: real (Mogadishu) war and virtual (NBA) war. Or was it the reverse? Mogadishu as the virtual war, with its electronic mapping of the geographic coordinates of Aidid's military base and TV headquarters (were they the same?) and its application of the laser weaponry of pure technology to achieve a virtual kill? And was the Suns/Bulls game, with its violent match-up of the god-like Jordan and the super-intense Barkley, complete with a brilliantly arrayed rhetoric of strategy, tactics, and logistics, the real war in the android hearts of the virtual population?

Or something different? Not virtual war versus real war, but the superannuation of war into an indeterminate doubling: *bimodern war*. In this case, the violent bombing of Mogadishu provided the cycle of primitive energy necessary to sustain the pure technology of NBA championship basketball. And the in-your-electronic-face basketball of Jordan and Barkley provided the tactical clues guiding the American air force as it flipped Mogadishu into the electronic trash-bin of a computer application: total aggressivity, electronic scanning, networked virtual simulation of the target population, and specular publicity. In this case, the night bombing of Mogadishu, under the sign of basketball tactics, issues in the use of AC-130H gunships as the military equivalent of 3-point shots (safe from grasping hands); and the "end-game" of Mogadishu displays all the finesse of a half-court press. Mogadishu as the real virtual sport? Why not? This was a sacrificial scene where an accidental range of victims is selected for purposes of enhancing the internal (telematic) moral cohesion of the home team (US/UN). Michael Jordan Mogadishu, then, as the first and best of all the virtual Air Force Generals. The only question remaining is this: was the disappearance of Mogadishu timed perfectly for the half-time of the NBA game: a final deft touch of bimodern war as the leading edge of promotional culture under the sign of pan-capitalism?

GOLD COAST HOT DOG

I'm writing this at Gold Coast Dog, a hot-dog joint at the corner of Clark and Dickens in Chicago. The place is filled with the sound-bites of CNN emanating from a big-screen color TV. That's the preferred ambient sight and sound in this place. Gold Coast Dog ain't a yuppie hangout. We're in "political" times. I'm performing an experiment. I will let whatever passes into me from CNN dictate my theme until something else from CNN displaces it.

Right now there's a feature on a study reporting that 80% of kids in American schools have been sexually harrassed in school. It seems like young men are exposing themselves to young ladies in the halls, in addition to insulting them. Fascist infantilism, one of the diseases of our time.

When they said "let it all hang out" they didn't have fascism in mind, they didn't have a vision of cocks on view in the halls. One expert says that you've got to separate boys being boys from serious sexual abuse. Another says that you shouldn't make teachers police gestures. Both are women. They smell fascism just like I do. The boys are fascist , but so is the liberal response of ever-more disciplinization. Liberal fascism versus fascist infantilism, which is one of the varieties, perhaps the most regressive, of the retro-fascism dominating the present public situation. In this case retro-fascism is boys who are deathly afraid of being men, who don't want to be men, who don't know how to be men (so they become parodies of masculinism). They rebel against manhood. They hate women for making them have *to take care of them, be nice to them.* They want to be taken care of. All fascists do. Terrorize and exterminate. Disciplinize to death. Take your choice. It's fascism all the way down.

This is not a bad way to image the post-liberal scene. Sexual bullies prowl the halls while the authorities cook up (plans for) more controls.

CNN moved on long ago. Something about stomach pains is on now. Popular medicine displaces popular sociology. I refuse to get involved.

THE BUNKER STATE

Consider those melancholic media scenes of Chinese refugees (jumping off grounded ships in New York harbor or discovered stuffed in San Francisco warehouses) who set foot on the shores of America only to find themselves imprisoned, and promptly expelled. They live in a virtual world between slave culture and forced expulsion. (Geographically) homeless, (economically) nomadic and (politically) preyed upon by predators, they are the representative sign of the endlessly circulating underclass in the political economy of virtual reality.

The ruling triad of pan-capitalism (Japan, Western Europe, and North America) maintain their economic hegemony by enhancing their adaptive capacity to the governing principle of the virtualized economy: *to stop (the nomadic body of) immigration.* In pan-capitalism, immigration is viewed as a purely parastical function that drains the social energies of an already evacuated political economy. In the eighteenth and nineteenth centuries, immigration could be encouraged, particularly in the United States, as a way of providing a mobile labor force through the relentlessly expanding commodity-form. Even in the mid-twentieth century, selective (political) immigration was permitted as a disciplinary strategy aimed at exposing, and thereby weakening, the closed-door carceral of socialist states. Now, however, at the end of the millennium, the game of immigration is up, just like a game of musical chairs that we thought would never end: we have entered the age of the bunker state.

The necessity of providing a mobile labor force for the manufacturing sector is achieved by arranging global free-trade zones (NAFTA, the European Community) for an endless repositioning of (American) manufacturing plants close to the cheapest (Mexican/Haitian) supply of labor on the market. Or the political mechanism of "most favored nation status" can be used to remake China as a standing (labor) reserve for the retail trade of the ruling triad of the empire of virtual reality. No longer is labor-value in search of a market for its sale, but now a virtualized market for coordinating global market positioning is in search of stay-at-home labor.

In pan-capitalism, immigration is a no-go zone: a nomadic quest in search of a better life that is not honoured because, with the eclipse of communism abroad and the degradation of the economy at home, immigration simultaneously loses both its moral justification and its economic appeal. The age of moral amnesia begins, in which refugees from dispossessed countries, from Romania to Haiti, are imprisoned in concentration camps, and then expelled, without the slightest ripple of public discontent because the policing of immigration fits perfectly the liberal ethic of "petty conveniences." It is a time of sacrificial immigration where refugees have a final value only as victims on the table of economic grievances by local populations. Witness the burning of the Turkish emigrant hostel in Germany by right-wing skinheads with the tacit consent of the German government (Kohl is courting the East German vote), and the enthusiastic applause of a majority of the population.

And those Chinese immigrants in New York and San Francisco? They are repeating the story of an earlier Chinese migration to America (to build the railway across the expanding frontier), but this time no immigrant workers are required to build the digital superhighway across the liquid space of virtual America. They are trapped in an historical loop that has gone out-of-synch: refugees from a Chinese society that is quickly regressing to the feudal days of war lords and despotic gang bosses. (Economic) penitents are literally thrown out of the sea at the feet of a Statue of Liberty that has gone out of (virtual) date.

They are the (televised) tombstone of the American myth of the expanding frontier: "Huddled masses" to be thrown back into the sea as unwanted body invaders of America in the age of virtual capitalism.

HIV PRISON CAMP

Call it whatever else you want, but an HIV prison camp is also retro-fascism. It all began under Reagan when Haitian boat people were shipped to an abandoned facility in upstate New York. Since then, the Haitians have been America's special scapegoats. The HIV prison camp in the Guantanamo Naval Base has been known about for a while. Clinton promised to close it during his campaign, but, in typical fashion, neglected to do so once he got elected. The camp contains 158 Haitian refugees, most of them HIV positive. Now Clinton will fulfill his campaign promise because U.S District Judge Sterling Johnson has ordered the camp shut down and he will not contest that ruling.

The Judge said of the inmates: "They live in camps surrounded by razor barbed wire. They tie plastic bags to the sides of the building to keep the rain out. [Gulag?] [They] have been subjected to predawn military sweeps as they sleep, by as many as 400 soldiers in full riot gear [state terrorism]. . . . . Simply put, they are merely the unfortunate victims of a fatal disease."

The HIV prison camp is the American pop-sociology nightmare come true. It is a never-on-TV horror story. Fascism does not yet simulate its negative environments. That is the next frontier—virtual punishment. These days fascists still want meat, even if it's tainted—especially if it's tainted. What about a prime-time docudrama on a day in the "life" of an HIV prison camp? We need a romantic angle.

SPANISH CATS AND THE BODY ELECTRIC

The fate of animals in Spain prefigures the fate of the virtual body. In the name of greater animal safety, Spanish cats and dogs must be either tattooed at birth or have a micro-chip surgically implanted in their skin. When found as strays on the city streets, their electronic history can be pulled up (from a distance) by roving scanners, and their owners traced. Spanish officials are now considering adding new data files to the encrypted micro-chips of these telematic cats and dogs: their medical history of vaccinations, records of sexual sterilization, and a history of (cat) offenses against the public order.

What happens now to virtualized animals in Spain anticipates the future of the electronic (sub-human) body. With this difference: the surgical implanting of a micro-chip in the virtual body will not be resisted, but welcomed, actually demanded, in the name of safety. What mother would not want her baby to be electronically identifiable from birth? Here, the tattoo of the concentration camps comes inside, and is electronically inscribed in the skin of the virtual body. Not only will micro-chips be used for electronic scanning, but molecular micro-computers straight from Silicon Valley will be inserted directly into the blood stream. Who does not want to be healthy? Who does not want to be warned in advance of the undetectable breakdowns of vital bodily organs? This is health fascism: the archiving of the medicalized body in the name of the preservation of good health. A virtual body, therefore, that emits a steady stream of electronic data about its identity, the health of its vital organs, its white blood cell count, the speed and circulability of its credit financing: like a spacecraft at the outer edge of the galaxy that beams digital radio messages about its electronic journey across the Milky Way.

The 1990s as the closing days of the slaughterhouse century. And Nietzsche's body vivisectionists? They are those gloating scientists from MIT and Harvard who performed radiation experiments on the "mentally retarded," and called it progress. Philosopher George Grant was correct when he predicted that the ethics of technological liberalism would be the ethics of the "petty conveniences" on the one hand, and radical injustice against the weak, the powerless, and the poor on the other. Such is the doubled language of cynical power at the fin-de-millennium. The virtual surveillance system has warped out of the bodies of those Spanish cats and dogs, and phase-shifted into the bloodstream of the virtual population of America.

TELEMATIC KITSCH AND COLD MURDER

It is difficult to orient one's ethical sensibility at the end of a century that oscillates wildly between telematic kitsch and cold murder. At one moment, you are blindsided by techno-euphorics announcing some further radical experiment in body virtualization, and then you turn the media page to read about murder squads composed of policemen slaughtering homeless children at night on the streets of Rio de Janiero, or Amnnesty International's report concerning the surgical removal of organs from the bodies of executed "criminals" in Taiwan and sold to the highest bidder on the international organ market. The Amnesty report also added that Taiwanese prisoners on death row are kept for months in special shackles (abattoirs do the same in the production of veal: don't hurt the meat), and that it is not improbable that bodies are selected for execution depending on the virtual demand for specific body parts: recombinant (organ) harvesting.

Virtualization for recliners on the one hand, and cynical murder on the other. Not a moral chasm of impossibility, but two deeply coterminous tendencies: virtualization as the murder of (telematic) flesh, and murder as the harvesting of the (human) remnant. Really, two forms of harvesting: one for the virtual class as it disappears into the matrix; and the other for the powerless as it is appropriated of its fleshly remainder. And all of this just as Camus predicted in *The Rebel*: a perfect union of metaphysical and historical rebellion in the slaughterhouse of a twenty-first century that has already been bleached of its meaning in advance. Beyond the revolt against God (murder in the name of justice) and beyond the rebellion against injustice (murder in the name of reason), we are the heirs of virtual rebellion. A revolt against the flesh which, parading in the doubled language of cynical seduction and cynical humiliation, spirals inwards as a rebellion against the will itself. No longer the will to power or even the will to powerlessness, but now the will to will-lessness: The telematic body delivers itself up stripped of intentionality (a floating politics), of morality (a recursive ethics for a mirrored world), of vision (for improved virtual optical sensors), and of a self (as the tour guide in Xerox Parc said: "Who needs a self anyway?"). A virtual rebel, the telematic body sums up in its pixel gestures, imaging-repertoire, and algorithmic (designer) skeleton the evacuation of the bowels of the flesh by the gnawing worm of the will to will-lessness. Not harvesting under the sign of use-value, but virtual harvesting for a combinatorial of motives: revenge against a "living insult" to the tourist trade (the children in Rio de Janiero); or a perfect alliance of profit-making (in freshly extracted organs) and state justice. The pleasure palace and the torture chamber, then, as the doubled sign of virtual rebellion. So then, some data intermissions from the electronic body.

INTERMISSIONS

Friendliness is for Rest-Stop Junkies

So you're driving down the data superhighway in a beautiful new computer console with an Intel Pentium chip under the hood. Your buddy in his Mac Power PC with its slow-poke Motorala RISC chip is fast receding in the rear-view mirror. But like the business report in the New York Times said: "Mac's got a heart...(it's) fuzzy friendliness", and the Intel chip has got flat-out acceleration. On the electronic highway, only speed counts: friendliness is for rest-stop junkies who have gone into terminal recline.

IMAX Memory

For the virtual class, the world outside may fade away, but it is instantly replaced by IMAX(ed) history. Giganticism is the special hallmark of the recycled imagery of the recombinant archive. Consider the immense popularity of IMAX, those bloated screens with their thunderous sound-effects for the resuscitation in mega-mode of all the detritus of the virtual history archive: IMAX at the Grand Canyon, IMAX in deep space, IMAX at MTV rock concerts, IMAX as the hologram of the White House(?).

IMAX is a perfect model of cyber-history as it recycles human remainders through the dead lens of telematic imagery. Here, the lacerations of organic flesh are filtered out, and the perverted image appears with a technologically constituted history of the human (telematic) species. Why visit the Grand Canyon, except to verify the negligibility of nature in the face of the real virtual wonder of the IMAX world? Images swell up to fill the available telematic horizon: they are resequenceable, interchangeable, and always perfectible. In recombinant history, the image is the real thing, and the real thing is only an illusion of virtualization. Giganticism of the screenal economy occurs in inverse proportion to the miniaturisation of human subjectivity.

Consequently, our telematic history: neo-segregation for the powerless, and neo-isolation in the electronic bestiary for the recliners. The stabilized image shatters, and suddenly we are plunged back into medievalism in virtual drag.

Tokyo De Sade

The Japanese have a better idea, and they are leading the way in the creation of a recombinant history fit for virtual life-forms in the twenty-first century.

I recently planned to visit the galactic empire of the Japanese sign to explore the will to virtuality. But I never went there because I never left here. I was intercepted on my way by a European TV video-maker, Stefaan Decostere, who, like a nomadic space traveller, beamed down one summer afternoon on one of his vectors around the global media-net. He had just completed an intensive seven-week "shoot" in Japan, filming twenty-five Japanese "fantasy worlds" in the same number of days: one fantasy world for every arc of the Japanese sun. Titled *Déja Vu*, the video traced the proliferating fantasy world of Japan where the citizens of the empire of the sign pump up their virtualized flesh with high-intensity five-day holiday junkets. See the perfect (one-to-one) replica of a Dutch village complete with cathedrals, canals and busy city streets. Live in an echanting simulacrum of Mexico (staffed by imported Mexican workers). Attend a Spanish fiesta. Visit the Alpha Hotel in Tokyo for a fantasy torture chamber of your choice. Resynch with traditional Japan by buying a condo in "Samurai Village", or, perhaps, visit the newest Shinto shrine with its tens of thousands of Buddha statues, each bedecked with a red ribbon honoring the departed spirit of an aborted fetus.

Little fantasy bubbles spread across the Japanese media-net for quick entries and exits: training sessions for the virtualization of the flesh. Simultaneously sites of relief from the rigid cultural coding of the Japanese techno-juggernaut and bucolic scenes of fun culture, the fantasy worlds are laced together by flashing screens displaying exactly the same story line: a threatening, real world imploding with violent catastrophes outside of the fantasy palaces. The peaceable kingdom of the Dutch fantasy world can immediately flip into its opposite: turbulent scenes of mass drownings and cities collapsing when the dikes break, As Decostre says: "The Japanese just want to do good. They don't understand why the rest of the world doesn't just adopt their fantasy fixes as the real (techno-ecological) thing." And so, a little Japanese boy appears on the scene to rescue the real world with a quick technological fix.

Japanese fantasy worlds are the end-game of the will to virtuality, a transition to nowhere occurring as virtualized flesh dumps into the electronic (memory) archive. Processed worlds are created for effortless action, where data bodies can actually become a fantasy of choice: Anne of Green Gables, Sade in Tokyo, hyper-Samurai. Not Disney World (which is always self-referential), Japanese fantasy worlds are brilliantly engineered models for better (technological) living. They are fantasy theme parks designed to be permanently lived in, and, after a decade or so, to be integrated into Japanese society as the new micropolitan regions of the future. Fantasy worlds, therefore, as genetically engineered suburbs, with their perfect mixture of personal adventure and high-tech performance, as the designer model for the genetically engineered (virtual) citizen of the future: fun culture and processed world.

Net Nerves

The Net is the nervous system of the electronic body. It cannot easily be destroyed because of its auto-immunity system. Shielded from natural disasters (earthquakes) and social meltdowns (nuclear war), the Net is a densely fibrillated ganglia of computer nervous tissue, 15,000 strong at the last count and exponentially increasing. Infected parts can be rapidly isolated from the organic whole, data can be regenerated, and T-cell anti-receptors in the form of worms and viruses can be "fingered" by system operators at the toggle of a (world-wide surveillance) switch.

Human history began much the same way. Pre-biotic organic mass washed up out of the ocean's vast spaces, flopped onto the beach, and began to mutate wildly as its cellular structure came alive, and drove to higher and higher levels of complexity and abstraction. In its wake, the Net splits out of the skull of human consciousness, flops onto the waiting digital beach, and nerve ganglia begin to spread like rhizomes across planetary space. Suddenly the Net begins to breathe, coughs a bit to clear its fluidless lungs, and goes online as the latest in the evolutionary chain of species-beings.

We straddle two competing life-forms: the data-net and the flesh-net. Which is real? The data-net as an auto-defense for the human species, an electronic shield that we have constructed to absorb the shock-waves of technological change for a human species that has gone into a shell turtle-like? Or the flesh-net as an artificial construct designed by the electronic kingdom to experience feelings for the baby body of the information net, while it comes to maturity? The data-net as an externalization of the human nervous system (McLuhan)? Or the flesh-net as a simulacrum of information? And what happens (to us) when the data-net and the flesh-net enter into the inevitable Darwinian struggle for scarce resources? Will post-human flesh be a body dump to be harvested by the data-net? Or is the information highway a great facilitator of human experience? Or both? Harvested flesh is an energizer for a data void that threatens to go hyper-spatial in the absence of bodies which act as uniform resource locators on the World Wide Web. And bodies are telematically accelerated by their downloading as archival information bases by the waiting data vat. Data flesh, then, as the topology of the body redesigned for fast ejection into the space of the millennium.

Body Dumps

Body Dumps? That is where flesh goes to be virtualized. Shopping malls, TV talk shows, computer consoles, fax machines, rock videos: all quick-time processing machines for harvesting the body of its organic juices, and draining bone and tissue into an indefinite spiral of telemetry. No longer a consumer model of economy, but an exterminatory one working in the language of harvesting. Not information but the large-scale archiving of body parts, dreams, and projects. And certainly not communication but a violent strategy of dissuasion for disappearing communication into serial data flows.

The ecstasy of exterminism. Enter the magnetic field of the body dump, and flesh is relieved of its history, scanned for its memories, and stored in a fashion file. That is the seduction of exterminism: to be relieved finally of responsibility for dragging around fleshly remainder. Like a game of musical chairs played at the digital level, the trick is not to get caught at the turn of the century in a localized space. The rest position is death, just because the body, local history, and fixed chronological time is the antithesis of the space-binding world of the data-net. In the game of the virtual class, when the music suddenly ends, you want to find yourself floating free in the data void, suspended beyond the ground(ing) referents of history, sex, consciousness, and power. Stranded on the beach with the virtual tide running out and your feet stuck in the muck of a referent: that is the story of the coming victims of virtuality.

Fuzzy Logic

I am sitting in Foufounes Electrique, an underground cyberpunk music bar in Montreal. I've a shooter in my hand, copies of Bruce Sterling's *Crystal Express* and Nietzsche's *The Will to Power* in my data bag, and my cyber-flesh is taking direct hits from the sound force-field of *Fuzzy Logic*, a group of digital music hackers who might drift along in nowhere sub-jobs by day, but who, when the moon comes up, hard-wire their multi-racks of synthesizers into the universal nervous system of wired culture. My skin splits open, fuzzy logic comes inside, and suddenly I'm riding the virtual snake. Not pushing through to the other side anymore (in the culture of seduction all sides are mirrored ellipses), but letting my mind follow the drift-currents of the tales incredible that I heard last night from other travellers on the virtual road: stories of "digital readouts available on the inside of your eyelids," of bar codes as "the mark of the beast of the apocalypse," and of a virtual economy, a wired culture where you actually become the bar code at the electronic check-out counter. The body electronic becomes processed data, infinitely fungible, always exchange-able, ever ready for circulation as an after-image in the circular flows of capitalism in its virtual phase, disappearing into technology.

A data globe dominated by the will to virtuality, where the body electronic is presented with this fateful choice: to recline into virtuality or to hack its way to digital freedom. I knew I didn't want to be a virtualizer reclining into the weak will of the (electronically) harvested body, so I picked up my data bag, rubbed Sterling and Nietzsche together again, and began to hack out this virtual tale of pilgrim's progress. Where will it end or has it even begun? I don't know, and I don't care. *Fuzzy Logic* is inside of me, I know, and I signal the waiter for another vodka shooter.

Taiwan Data Heaven

Red Rock comes on-line. He tells me about a great new surfing destination in Taiwan. Seems that it is the largest data storage dump in the virtual world: unlimited FTPing territory, a kind of cyber-world where a hacker could put down roots. It is comparable to Turner's frontier thesis of the promised land, but rather than stopping at the physical edge of continental U.S.A., you keep on vectoring towards the new horizon of the rising sun. Taiwan as the geographic edge of virtual America. Everyone in California has hard-wired their bodies, and are heading out for the interstitial coordinates of the Taiwan FTP site. I can't resist the impulse, and so I head out too. Before I disappear into the Net, I leave a note behind saying that if I haven't been seen for a day, send a cyber-search party, but be careful because I'm not sure what crash events await unsuspecting travellers in the East.

The Taiwan FTP site was everything I could have hoped for. Tetra-gigabytes of data: gleamingly arranged, sub-sonic vectors of information banks arrayed against a background sky of liquid crystal blue, pure data heaven. It's all there for the asking, and the Taiwanese sysops are true to the word that has been put out on the Net about them—"the friendliest folks I ever met," said Moog from Amsterdam. A free-fall into data, almost heavy with its gravitational weight. Less like an FTP site than a gigantic data harvesting-machine, the Taiwan FTP site aimlessly strips the media-net of its content, archiving the human story into its humming machinery.

Red Rock signals me to get off at the freeway exit to alt. sex, Taiwanese style. I flip on my encryption sensors, and head straight for this new file horizon. And it's weird. A vast data storage bank for cyber-sex: bondage rituals, stories of sado-masochism that make you understand for the first time the pure aesthetics of disciplining of the flesh, stories of virtual bodies that merge together to the sound of crackling (electronic) body static as two neuro-skins that would be one make love against a crystalline background of data walls.

It's perfect that the world's largest data management base should be zoned away in Taiwanese electronic space. Data has always been future to our past, and pure data is the East as the end of western history, and the beginning of virtuality. The West, then, is just material for more history: archiving and data management in real-(on-line)-time in Taiwanese cyberspace as the telematic form assumed by the horizon of the virtual history file. And something else too. Taiwan was one of the first of the genuinely recombinant societies to surface from the ruins of World War II. Not authentically Taiwanese (after its colonization by the fleeing Chinese nationalists) and certainly not pure Chinese, Taiwan was always fated to be a unique historical mutation. A key part of global virtual economy, with its early restructuring by multinational corporations in search of cheap labor and even cheaper taxes, Taiwan has long been prepared as a data management system for sifting through all of the detritus of the virtual world. It has become a storage dump created by the intricate web of the MNC's and policed by the aging nationalist autocracy for downloading all of the electronic signals sent out by the pure instrumental activism of the rest of the globe.

And this is just as it should be because when life has no history, then data is the only sign of cynical power. Could this isolated Taiwanese FTP site be that key node where the genealogy of the Chinese mind is grafted onto telemetry, and the result is an infinite circularity of digital history?

But then, I'm a lurker here, a traveller in virtual Taiwan who always wanted to visit the East, and now doesn't have to bother.

The Internet Body

We are the Internet Body, and it's too slow. Internet flesh is an electronic nomad that travels the slipstreams and gateways of the digital superhighway. Requiring mass feedings of data from all the on-line services and sucking up the congealed mass of data overload into its flesh ports, the Internet Body has telemetried consciousness moving at the advance edge of the information network. Demanding the liquidation of information and the end of communication, the Internet Body wants only pure signal. It needs to reassure itself that its virtual presence is only an illusion and that it might be dumped again into the gravity well of the flesh. A master of digital extremes, the Internet Body craves speed and inertia: speed for vectoring across the electronic frontier, and inertia for moving towards the end of information and the beginning of stochastic culture. A virtual traveller, the Internet Body is never interested in the journey, only in its destination: the beginning of the endless ritual of data senses mapped by the curving grid of stochastic space.

Once upon a time, we might have had Rousseau's "sovereign self," Locke's "possessive individual," Stirner's "autonomous ego," but now the Internet Body is their digital successor. A virtual self with a digital ego that knows only the Internet as its electronic leviathan. One big extopian culture marked by the disappearance of flesh into the infinite telemetry of signalling capacity, and the vanishing of the physics of AI into the storage dump of the wired body. The body electronic as a violent, but no less fascinating, recursive space: all signalling skin/all memoried telemetry. Cyber-saliva dripping from the beaks of all those virtual seagulls as they scavenge the dump of downloaded flesh.

The Internet is the skin of the body electronic. A living bio-technical organism wired with virtual communication to such a point of excess and immediacy that it becomes a living cellular creature, a data membrane stretched around the globe like a pulsating nervous system.

Building the (Electronic) Railway into the 21st Century

In Sergio Leone's movie, *Once Upon a Time in the West*, Cheyenne says to the railway baron: "I can always find you. You've left your slime trail, the railway tracks, across the land." That could be the triumphant retort of the Internet. Like at the end of the nineteenth century, the final days of the twentieth century witness the building of a new slime trail, the digital superhighway, across the global landscape into the next millennium.

Intervertisments

In the good old days the data highway used to be a big blue void: cold as ice with a sunny horizon, and not even a cloud in the electronic sky. But that was then, and this is now. The information highway has become data trash. Video billboards are everywhere: They are called *Intervertisments*. They seduce the digital eye, and reduce the monotony

of the trip. Unlike billboards in the age of pavement, these advertisements are injected directly into the veins of the post-flesh body like bar
codes burned into flesh. Who says information is free? Data is dragged
back from its dream of infinite acceleration into spherical space: pleasure
domes for tired digital bodies. You flip out of hyper-drive and head for the
next exit when you spot the sign for McSoft burgers, the Intel food of
choice at the gas station right up the road.

Virtual Evil

The virtual class possesses a new body type modelled on the requirements of life in the age of the post-human. No longer the body human,
but it is the virtual class as cybernauts who register in the flesh every
twitch of techno-culture. Always hystericized because driven from
within by feelings of hyper-anxiety over demands for the new in techno-
culture, and partly inferior before the technical momentum of the virtual
reality machine, cybernauts are perfect nihilists. A technologically-
steered class, they face outwards with an overwhelming sense of contempt, but interact with each other on the basis of real confusion and fear
over their constantly changing status in the commercial command
hierarchy of techno-culture.

In *Beyond Good and Evil*, Nietzsche provided the encryption key to
deciphering the psychology of cybernauts. For Nietzsche, good and evil
are interchangeable terms, flip sides of the same doubled sign of nihilism.
Map *Beyond Good and Evil* onto the spatial coordinates of the virtual
class, and what surfaces is a study of exterminism with a smiling face. No
longer is there an easily recognizable evil under the sign of nostalgic
signifiers, but now a new glittering rhetoric of virtual evil.

Virtual Evil? That is cybernauts as the sign of the beast with two easily
identifiable marks burnt on their electronic flesh. First, the mark of
forgetfulness, as cybernauts systematically expunge from their world-view
any account of the human costs associated with the coming to be of the
technological dynamo. And secondly, the mark of *techno-fetishism*, as
cybernauts transform their cyber-bodies and cyber-consciousness into
living registers of emergent technologies. Total repression and total
valorization, then, as the twin signs of virtual evil.

NIETZSCHE' S (CRASH) AMERICA

Here the worms of vengefulness and rancor swarm *Let the Dead Bury the Living* Here the air stinks of secrets and concealment *Let the Dead Bury the Living* Here the web of the most malicious of all conspiracies is being spun constantly *Let the Dead Bury the Living* How much sugary, slimy, submissiveness swims in their eyes *Let the Dead Bury the Living* The virtuous: how they crave to be hangmen *Let the Dead Bury the Living* Criminals put on judges robes at night and slip out of their cells to commit murder in the name of justice *Let the Dead Bury the Living* Our nihilists: they seek revenge on the weak for their own botched and bungled instincts *Let the Dead Bury the Living* Let us have fresh air, fresh air and keep clear of the hospitals of music *Let the Dead Bury the Living* Someone must be to blame for my feeling ill *Let the Dead Bury the Living.*

CHAPTER SIX

VIRTUAL (PHOTOGRAPHIC) CULTURE

Virtual-Photography

Imaging technology reveals the sufferings of the flesh in virtuality at the same time that it co-constitutes the negligibility of the flesh.

Virtuality was there with the first photograph: photographs are either scenes or event-scenes—they are windows, not on the world, but always on virtuality. We apologize in advance for repeating the conventional wisdom of academic photographic studies about the nature of the photo: it is a flat image, almost never on an ordinary perceptual scale and never displaying the colors of ordinary perception. Yet from the start, with William Henry Fox Talbott, the inventor of photography, the technology was being called a "window on the world" or, as Talbott put it, a "pencil of nature." The pencil-of-nature idea persists, held and disseminated in a thoroughly cynical way through a mediascape that refutes it with every new photographic image. The photograph was the first techno-virtual space, staged more than 150 years ago—all of technological virtuality has grown from this minimal, flat (event-)scene space to the VR-hologram. Movies and videos come in between.

Window on the world? Not only is the space of the photograph not perceptual space (VR tries to fix that), but most photographs are in some way staged. Indeed, photography is the seminal recombinant imaging form. Put anything together in the range of a camera and you have an event-scene. If that is not good enough you can cut apart and recombine negatives, air brush and color, and perform any other kind of alteration you can think of, keeping as much or as little as you wish of the illusion of "reality" associated with a photo taken according to realist conventions.

The great bastion of photography is advertising. From the word go, photographers were staging scenarios and experimenting with "darkroom magic." When mass photo reproduction technologies came in the photo took over and expanded advertising by virtualizing it and making it the prime and paradigmatic agent of virtualization. Advertising is recombinance disciplined only by the ceaseless effort of pan-capitalism to seduce or bully purchasing power. Anything goes if it might make a sale. Meanwhile the advertising photo creates virtual worlds that seduce and inflame the will to virtuality. Virtuality sells itself more than it sells "the product." The product is a cynical excuse for the need of reclining life for the seductive environment of advertising and its hyper-saturation of (event-)scenes (photos). Pan-capitalism is the way that reclining flesh pays itself for virtuality.

The photo is not a slice of the perceptual world. Even the photo that most closely fulfills the conventions of standard realism is a "reasonable facsimile" of what the eye might have seen. As a simulation of the enframed perceptual field, what the photo loses in its flatness is partly recupterated by its ability to seduce the illusion of the contents of the perceptual world or of a fantasy world that appears as though it might be perceptual. This seduction is the great strength of photography as a virtualizing medium. The state of present technology with respect to virtualization is this: virtual-reality technology is on the way to generating a reasonable facsimile of perceptual space but has not yet been successful in generating reasonable facsimiles of perceptual content; whereas the photographic media cannot simulate perceptual space (they do not surround and englobe—enframe—perception), but they do present credible simulations of perceptual content.

Something that is obviously not the perceptual world of the flesh but that can cynically be taken to be of the latter, and at the same time humiliates the flesh—that is the advertising photograph, the visual diet of the reclining eye. If the reclining eye is a voyeur, it is a cynical pervert and an accomplice in the humiliation of the flesh of which it is an organ. Advertising photography in magazines reveals the aesthetics of the will to virtuality. The photographic images are smooth, clear, and sharply focused, presenting an event-scene that is more precise and glossy than any scene ever is for enframing perception. This is an ideal of vision that could only be actualized for the flesh if it existed perceptually in the environment of magazine photography, which surely will be the direction taken by VR technology: not a simulation of the "ordinary" perceptual world, but a magazine world. The flesh will then be able to contemplate itself as magazine flesh—smooth, glossy, and clear.

The "lived body" under the control of the will to virtuality arranges its own humiliation through the slick magazine. Advertising photography produces more abuse value than any other pan-capitalist practice. It is not a matter of convincing the flesh that it should buy some product to make it accord with an impossible image or even to associate the sizzle with the dog food, but to train the flesh for virtuality by cynical seduction and chronic humiliation. Purchasing the product pays for the abuse value of the advertising photograph. Advertising photography: the fascination of humiliation.

The reclining eye has lost any sense of the difference between the advertising photograph and what it sees in enframed perception. That does not mean that the reclining eye confuses photographic space with general perceptual space, but that it no longer cares or notices that they are different. Surrealism runs rampant on the slick pages and is greeted with blinks. The same people who function in the noise machine to fight "culture-wars" against postmodernist photography or who express bewilderment, incomprehension, and injury when they see it are nonchalant about the (post-)modern antics of magazine-advertising photography. They are generally obedient organisms in training for virtuality, complicitous in the will to virtuality with a cynical wink.

Advertising never cared for any rules. As pure recombinance it never paid fealty to any genre conventions, either Philistine or avant-garde. It would be earnest, kitschy, high-brow, middle-brow, low-brow, reassuring, shocking, challenging, narcotizing, transgressive, and any combination of the above at once: pure recombinance. Consider the *Newsweek* issue of July 12, 1993. On the front cover a little yellow band in the upper right-hand corner announces "Free Trade: Why It's Good for You." Under the *Newsweek* masthead, in white letters on a red band, is a toned black-and-white shot, taken from behind, of Clinton, standing in a meditative pose, seeming to be reading something in front of a door opening out into a garden. To his right, on a small table, is a sculpture of what might be a bucking bronco ridden by a triumphant cowboy. Clinton is what Barthes called the *studium* of the image, its obvious subject. The sculpture is Barthes's *punctum*, the detail that reverses, subverts, deconstructs, and supplements the image. Clinton is before us, as cynical a sign as Madonna. Mr. Sensitive Policy Analyst, Rough Rider of Mogadishu. Black-and-white gives it dignity, the majesty of a dead technology that is now a "fine-art" form. Toning gives it "class." You can still hear people extolling the superiority of black-and-white. Cynical nostalgia. The headline on the cover in white lettering reads: "Exclusive: Seven Days: A Week in the Life of the President." At the lower left of the cover is the caption: "Thursday, June 24, 4:45 p.m." Photo-Clinton is having a Warholian moment. This is the noise machine. He is being hyped (massaged) in subdued black-and-white by the crooning machine.

The above is propaganda photography for the virtual liberal nation-state/empire. We find out inside that it was taken by a nameless White House staff photographer. This Clinton is a sensitive New Ager, attuned to technocracy, and working hard and thoughtfully to see to it that the best is done for us (that we are led tranquilized into the virtuality for which we crave). But make no mistake. That bronco tells us that he is everyone from Big-Stick Teddy to Give 'em Hell Harry to General George of the Gulf.

We see Clinton from behind, his bent head disclosing his profile. His hair is not as puffed as usual, the angle of the shot and his suit take away his chubbiness. We do not see the crudity and slackness of the recliner that comes out in frontal head shots of Clinton. Catching him from behind does two things at once: he both becomes a little vulnerable, bringing him down to and even beneath us (we could take him by surprise—indeed, that's what the camera seems to have done, given us a look through Sartre's keyhole); but he also is made distant and superior: he is making decisions. The photo is meant to seem as though it was not posed. It does not matter whether it was. Clinton exists in a photographic-photographed environment. He has adapted to that environment and has become a resource base for imaging, an element of the Diorama Presidency, a series of *tableaux vivants* made to be photographed. He has his back turned to us. Big Brother is Watching Policy (and you are watching him). Only it isn't him at all: It's Photo-Clinton. A virtual media-event.

This is where Clinton's free-fall has been arrested in July 1993, due presumably to some judgment, deliberate or not, within the noise machine that it would be more damaging to the interests of the virtual class to bash Clinton than to hype him (for the moment). *Newsweek's* cover depicts a media-generated pseudo-event-scene: understated-hype-propaganda.

Advertising takes over on the back cover with the recombinant photograph. Is it still true that what is good for GM is good for the country? That mismanaged dinosaur corporation, stung by Perot, occupies the back cover with an ad for the fascist power machine: The Chevy Blazer. As the headline says, "Everyone Can Use More Power, Friends, and Money." Especially reclining bodies, filled with ressentiment, who get their kicks taking a simulacrum of an armored vehicle on the streets. On the top half of the page is a photo-montage of the Power Machine against the background of a birch forest. The background image is a black-and-white shot of a strand of trees—a fine-art photograph by John Sexton. In the foreground is a standard glossy color image of the Blazer, attributed to no one. Here is the after-image of the recombinant commodity—a "product" first transformed into a standard commodity-image and then transported into a world of fine-art. The entire image is a recombinant sign, announcing that this Blazer belongs to virtuality, to John Sexton's attenuated, even decomposing image of trees, unconventionally "realistic," a quiet wilderness fit only to be populated by virtual bodies. Come to the etherealized, attenuated, bleached-out virtual forest where your Blazer sits ready to blast through the virtual trees. Only your photograph can ever get there.

Advertising is a fall into sin from the state of grace of virtuality. There are more virtual cars inside *Newsweek*. Advertising is a massive defensive armature created by the mediascape to win back virtualized flesh to the logistics of desire. BMW has a two-page spread dominated by a one-shot photo- drama. The headline reads: "It's Pouring Rain and an On Coming Vehicle Has Jumped the Yellow Line. Quick, Choose Your Luxury Car." The photo is dominated by "The Ultimate Driving Machine" coming around a corner out of the darkness, headlights burning and wheels turned toward the shoulder. A shadowy figure can barely be seen behind the windshield in the driver's seat. At the far right is the *punctum*, a blurred, spinning wheel and the fragment of a hood on a line toward the side of the BMW. It could be The Blazer! Virtual car wars.

But the whole scene takes place in an unworldly blue-violet light. Except for some drops on the hood of the BMW and some puddles on the shoulder there is no sign of a tempest. Everything is inert, even the spinning wheel. This is not an action shot, but a diorama shot. Indeed, it is peaceful; always already dead. Regressive yet projective, anxious yet serene, nostalgic yet hyperreal, advertising is like a plasmic bio-net arching across the invisible (barely visible) skin of the virtualized body as it follows its destiny to crash speed. The virtual crash is always but never: it is an inert crash. The photo shows a Diorama ready for the Smithsonian on the "Nervous Nineties," a hundred years from now.

The image subverts the headline. The headline is a hook to win back the virtual flesh. The image shows the already virtualized body, the body on the other side, too far gone to be reclaimed. Only a deep, dark bluish-violet shadow shows, a spot on the windshield on the virtual road. This body always crashes and never crashes. This ad is a sunshine report on events in virtual space. It is peaceful crashing there in the land of blue-violet light. Maybe this photo would have won a prize if it had been submitted to a juried show as the self-portrait of a postmodernist art photographer.

The last ad to visit in Newsweek is a single-page scare- kitsch-cute-hype for Public Television—a cynical recombinant sign at the service of virtual liberalism. Return to Clinton. The first thing you see, filling the bottom two-thirds of the page is a cute baby boy in a diaper aiming a remote-control straight at your face. The small headline in black letters at the top of the page reads: "Learning tool or loaded weapon?"

Here is the virgin flesh, the telematic baby, pointing this thing at you. Is this baby going to turn you on or zap you off the face of the hospice? Is this baby going to keep you in a nice hospice or is this baby going to put you in a nursing home that is even worse than the HIV Prison Camp? The baby has a look of intent wonder on its face. It could go either way. As virtual body, you could be disppeared by baby at any moment. And brought back. Why not take you into a studio and spend a few weeks videotaping you in every possible position and expression, and then just kill you off? They could give miles of videos of you to baby, who could then recombine them or blow you off at whim.

The cute little telematic baby—the greatest threat, the archetypal and paradigmatic nightmare of a debilitated will to live overgrown with the cancerous will to virtuality. "Don't zap me. Please don't zap me!. . . Zap me, please." We have seen the future. Virtualized bodies for virtualizing zappers. Baby works *through* the mediascape but never gets out, and we are also trapped there, in the telematic carceral; and maybe that's what we want. The remote control as telematic murder, brought to you by Public Television, whose motto we read is: "Keep us in mind," a hypnotic suggestion parading as cute.

The entire ad is a recombinant-cynical sign. Dead ideology for flesh seduced by therapy: look at all the good you will be doing (your) kids by sending them to Public TV, where they will be prepared for the "university of life." Precious, cute, kitschy, smarmy, and even Reaganesque. Then that baby points the zapper at you.

The baby is taken against a dark blue background—a conventional baby picture that you could get at Sears. Everything about the image is conventional except for that zapper. Only Public Television can save the next generation for the service of aging, reclining flesh. Watch out if they're not on Sesame Street. (Dead) power comes out of a zapper in a baby's hands.

Our perusal of the photos in *Newsweek*, July 12, 1993, comes to a close with a shot from the cover story, "Seven Days." One of the two largest photos in the piece is the only one of Hillary. The caption reads: "Hillary Rodham Clinton, taping a video tour of the White House, has retooled her image." On the left we see Hillary from the side standing apart in a large living room. At the far right a knot of technicians is grouped around video equipment and lights: telematic Hillary.

The photographer has emphasized the agony of the video shoot for the subject. Hillary is being scanned for images—she exists to be a resource base for image technology. She has been photographed from a distance so that she appears lost in the space that she occupies, at a distance that excludes community with those who are "testing" her (Benjamin) with the equipment. Except for the cameraman who points the camera (which looks like an assault rifle) straight at her, the techies seems to be oblivious to her presence; they either go about their work or watch the cameraman.

Hillary stands there, at the behest of the mediascape, a virtualizing body conducting a virtual tour. She is wearing a simple suit. We could see her at a church social, the minister's wife. She has that look of stressed discomfort that appears on the faces of the subjects of a shoot after they have been positioned and scanned for a while, and are finally becoming aggravated, depleted, dejected, and distressed. Her hand is clutched tensely into a fist. Hillary is going through a body procedure, just as if she were in a hospital or a torture chamber, but in this case there is no intent to cure her or to humiliate her directly, but to extract images from her, to virtualize her.

Hillary, as another recombinant-cynical sign. The "health-care czar" and partner of the President has "retooled" her image and appears now as the "traditional First Lady," another retreat in the reclining Presidency of Clinton: retro-nostalgia—"I can do a good Pat Nixon." Straight from the fashion file. It was on June 24 that the camera caught Clinton meditating in the company of the bronco. That same day Hillary was being virtualized for the virtual White House tour. Wait a second. I think I see two bucking broncos on a table in the far right-hand corner of the photo. What's going on? New Age cowboys and cowgirls on the telematic ranch?

**

Advertising photography was recombinant from its inception. At its beginning, in the 1920s, it was part and parcel of avant-garde modernism. Indeed, advertising photography in the 1920s was hyper-modern, adding commercial aims and moves to the modernist pastiche, thereby forever killing "art." Et tu, photography? All that remained for the postmodernists to do was to bring advertising (back) into "art," to (re-)appropriate it, in a recursive and cynical movement.

We see that cynical recursive movement in extreme form in the photo-art of Ellen Brooks. Brooks is a practitioner of postmodern techno-photography, the most distinctively yuppie photographic genre, populated by New Age souls with bad consciences. Her practice involves so many technical complications that no weekend snapshooter could ever imagine going through the process. Make no mistake. This is art. Nobody but an artist would do it, if only because the capital investment is so great. These works need buyers and galleries—the capitalist art-net is a necessary condition for their existence. Yet they are supposed to be subversive of advertising at the very moment that they are being advertised.

Ellen Brooks's practice: She appropriates images from house-and-garden magazines, rephotographs them, paints over them, and then photographs them through a screen. Her aim in performing this recombinant processing is to produce images that subvert the visual language of advertising by overturning hierarchies of signification. The results, however, are the reverse of Brooks's stated intentions. Her large color images radiate an impressionistic beauty which, far from subverting the codes of the commercial landscape myth, aestheticize them, provoking a tantalized sensation. Advertising has appropriated Brooks's art in the act of her appropriation of advertising. Brooks's art is hype for advertising, as cynical a commodity as there can be. She seduces you into advertising through her hype that parades as critical art. This is the art of the yuppie recliner.

Take the 58-inch by 49-inch "Front Entry" which shows a house in the woods on what looks like a snowy night. All is calm, all is bright. You expect to see Bing Crosby come by at any moment singing Christmas carols. Cool neon blues and greens are counterpointed by glowing orange windows. This cool, but sensuous, vision of the suburban home and hearth, served up in low resolution, has the feel of egg nog on a winter evening. You could just about eat the picture. This is art that promotes advertising and relies on advertising to promote it. Such is incestuous art-advertising: cynical nostalgia for the virtual spaces of house-and-garden photos that parade as criticism of the commercial myth of the suburbs. Here, deconstruction-transformation becomes a purely recursive process. For reclining life, advertising always wins. Art after it is dead.

Back in the 1920s art and advertising were naively incestuous inside the virtual space of the photograph. What are we to make of Ringl and Pit (Greta Stern and Ellen Auerbach)? They were Bauhaus photographers who opened up a commercial studio where they infused their assignments with modernist experimentation. There did not seem to be any contradiction for them between their sensitive portraits of Berthold Brecht and their ad photos promoting shampoo. Indeed, they were virtuosi of the disappearing/recombinant resource body.

In one of their shampoo ads a female mannequin holds a bottle of the product in her hand. A closer look reveals, however, that the hand is human. All body transactions are possible in virtual space. The intrusion of the (virtualized) flesh into Ringl's and Pit's remorselessly contrived scene creates a visual shock: shock-therapy for body nostalgia. It also draws attention to the bottle, fulfilling its commercial aim. But the surreal trick that Ringl and Pit have played also deconstructs the ad through the Derridian *pharmakon*. Does this bottle contain a magic elixir that transports the virtualizing flesh into virtuality or does it contain the poison that turns flesh into kitsch? Panic cuteness from the Bauhaus back in the 1920s.

Twenty years later advertising photography had become a modernist genre with its own conventions. Among the leading fashion and product photographers was Horst P. Horst, who has made his career in *Vogue*. Horst was one of the major figures in making fashion photography an art of seduction. He has used all the resources of avant-garde modernism to create fantasy worlds of cool passion where glamour dominates desire. Glamour is seductive. It is the product-effect of lights, props, makeup, and a look elicited from the virtualized face. Glamour exists to hype the virtual space. Just like the red Blazer in John Sexton's woods, Horst's women and products are not for the organic body but for the virtualized body: one must be virtualized to be in their world.

The look of Horst's women and products is elegant, combining sculptural form and classical poses with romantic suggestiveness, conjuring up a world for the reclining flesh in which it is too imperfect to live. Horst's elegance is remorseless. It is not yet cynical enough that Horst could keep from barfing it out.

In 1941 Horst managed without too much fanfare to do what Ellen Brooks claimed that she was trying to do. In "Surreal Beauty Cream" a flask, a container, and a mortar and pestle have been placed on a surface. A woman's hand holding a waxy rose dangles over a partition. Ugly wads of the "beauty cream" are stuck and smeared among the other objects. This image actually conveys disgust. We are witnessing the metastasizing product, the product as a cancer on the commodity, stripped of use value and exchange value, and retaining only abuse value. The product has become its own nemesis, turning against the glamour on which reclining bodies, stimulated by the will to virtuality, feed, and, therefore, turning against advertising photography itself. The product here is out of control (as it always already is). Horst's surreal beauty cream is a crash product, an anti-product, the nightmare of advertising, the (virtual) consumer's nightmare. Just like the baby aiming the remote control at us, Horst's beauty cream is a terror of virtuality.

Abuse value comes in many forms. The virtual body is subject to every possible transaction and recombination. Bodies are taken into the mediascape, recombined there, and made into recombinant sign-commodities. They are then further transformed as they are exchanged in networks of practices. Abuse value is added at each stage.

Richard Misrach is an able photographer who has gained a reputation for his vivid color shots of flooded towns in the west. Like Brooks, he is challenging conventions, in his case of the landscape, in the name of a cause (environmental consciousness). Misrach's flood images are notorious for their beauty. It is another case of the cynical sign, of yuppie recline, of having it both ways, of aestheticizing the criticized object: aestheticizing criticism. But at least Misrach's photographs are beautiful.

Anyway, Misrach was out west on one of his photographic expeditions, wandering around a nuclear test range, when he happened upon two *Playboy* magazines that had been used for target practice. The bullet-riddled mags fascinated him, so he took them home and photographed their pages in the luscious color that is his signature.

The semiotic layering of these images is Escher-like. First, there is the magazine photo, already a virtuality. Then there is that photo macerated by the bullets. Finally, there is Misrach's photo of the macerated photo, which restores the supremacy of the advertising aesthetic of the glossy magazine. This constant reprocessing illustrates the imminent reversibility of the (cynical) sign from virtual life to virtual sacrifice to virtual resurrection. *Virtual life.* Madonna looks at us seductively from the page of a clean *Playboy*. *Virtual sacrifice.* Seductive Madonna is shot up and pocked up with holes. No blood, of course—this is virtuality. Sign sacrifice (Madonna truly now is a *sacrificial* sign). *Virtual resurrection.* No need to restore virtual Madonna to the state of her initial appearance; she can be virtually resuscitated by smoothing her out again on photographic paper. With the pocks in her cheeks she is more interesting than she has ever been before—the virtual material-girl has survived the virtual bullets as a recombinant-mutant—virtually-dead/virtually-resurrected— still-as-always-seductive, recombinant Madonna.

Misrach can also show you a jolly male-bonding group sharing some vodka blasted away and Ray Charles's cheek ripped to shreds. The only one who survived intact, strange to say, was Ollie North, headlined as "The Sexiest Shredder." Misrach also snapped him, in all his virtual integrity, for virtual posterity. Virtual life, death, and resurrection form a closed loop in Misrach's *Playboy* series. By rehabilitating the humiliated image he has shown the impossibility of tragedy in virtuality. The most wounded image can be made whole by making it slick again. Abuse value as the resurrection of the humiliated image.

What about the triumph of consumer capitalism over the war machine? Not so fast. The resurrection is of a *sacrificial* sign. Misrach's series is deeply cynical. Those bullet holes only add to the seduction. Nothing would be fascinating to us if just the damaged *Playboy* were in front of us. Everyone has seen trashed magazines. By his resurrection-effect Misrach has not only aestheticized wounded virtual Madonna, but has also aestheticized the violence done to her (military-entertainment). We are more excited by Madonna with holes in her face than with the original. Misrach has upstaged the ad by letting the war machine into it on favorable terms. Now that Madonna is safely smoothed out on a seamless photographic surface, not so damaged that she cannot still smile at us, we are free to be titillated by the violence, now safely mummified. Richard Misrach: provisioner of images of virtual resurrection to reclining life.

Robert Heinecken is another able "photo-artist" who upstages ads. Heinecken does a lot of flying and while he is up in the air he peruses magazines and tears the ad pages out of them. When he gets home he puts the pages on color photographic paper and exposes them to light. The resulting photograms are seamless images of both sides of each page that resemble double exposures. The images retain all the elements of the magazine advertising-photography aesthetic, but reveal recombinant culture as no ad ever does, and are visually complicated in ways that ads never are.

An ad for condoms ("smart sex in the '80s") appears in four images, fused with ads for microwave dinners, "cool and classy fashions," pregnancy tests, and Bloomingdales. Heinecken punctures the illusion of seriality (separation) by making the horizon of sign possibilities simultaneous. Again as in Brooks's and Misrach's cases the images are aestheticized and function as hype for advertising. The attempts by "artists" to make art out of advertising invariably become promotions for advertising, which draws everything that touches it into its seductive games of recombinance in a mediascape in which everything is always dying, crashing, and always being resurrected. Horst, not an artist, but a celebrity fashion photographer, succeeded in subverting advertising by being disgusting. There is a lesson there.

Heinecken's recombinant ads-art sometimes succeeds in revealing some nightmares of virtuality. "Patterned Faces" shows two images of grotesque orgies of female faces with their red lips crowding in on each other. Some of the heads seem to be coated with slime. This is the hell

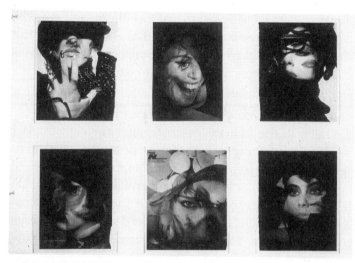

Robert Heinecken
Overlapped Faces

of recombinant fashion where designer bodies grow into each other, oozing cosmetic slime. There is something of a virtual Hieronymous Bosch in "Surreal Beauty Cream" and "Patterned Faces." These images introduce us to the monstrosities that are always lurking in virtuality. Sade's castle as photo studio.

Art photography that is critical of advertising and appropriates it finds its only margin of independence from advertising by producing images that appear to be ads but that would never appear as ads. Such photography broadens the boundaries of recombinance, showing greater possibilities for virtuality than capitalist enterprises are willing to entertain. At the same time, this photography exists within pan-capitalism and is one of its most cynical expressions. It is the aborted and always-already co-opted criticism carried on by reclining life. Hype-crit. Crit-hype.

Why not shut down signification altogether as Robert Metzger does? Metzger turns his video camera on the screen of a color video monitor and captures the feedback. Then he digitizes the "raw images," enhances their color, and prints selected frames. The resulting photos swell within a rarified world of electronic waste and visual static—what appears when the TV image breaks down.

In "Force = Mass × Acceleration" three dark-blue blobs seem to sail over a deep-blue pool flecked with yellow points of light, and across a baby-blue and pink sky. Metzger has shown us the last trace of the vanishing product as it gets sucked into the recombinant commodity— as good a look at the purely telematic vision as we are likely to get.

Scenes from the Virtual Beach: Amnesic's Playground

What is the quality of the human condition after the catastrophe? What mode of subjectivity emerges that makes it possible for people to sustain themselves in the absence of the great unifying principles of experience, in the absence, that is, of the referential totalities? Or do human beings, after the catastrophe, enter into the novel historical condition of "amnesic playgrounds," where identity dissolves into listless waiting, where the dominant color signs are purple and black (the mythological colors of mourning), and where perspective itself mutates into an endless cancellation of inside and outside. In post-catastrophe time, have we become celebrants of amnesia, agents of forgetfulness to such an intensity that we are no longer capable of questioning the horizon within which we are enucleated?

The question of amnesia, of the forgetfulness of post-catastrophe personalities, is put most evocatively by the artist, Edmund Alleyn.[1] In Alleyn's paintings, the cancellation of personality is complete. Here it is no longer a question of the calculative egoism of classical liberalism, but of the appearance of the "dissolved egoism" of virtual culture. No longer does a lived relationship between culture and remembrance exist, but the eclipse of memory is itself the hallmark of the eclipse of the individual. Indeed, to meditate on Alleyn's painterly descriptions of the non-time of the post-catastrophe is suddenly to be situated in the presence of absence as the defining moment of contemporary culture.

Here the subject-matter is leisure culture, the privileged medium is photography, the dominant color signs are violet and black leavened with X-ray scans of ultra-red, and perspective is reduced to the optical flatness of a moving photographic negative. Alleyn presents a painterly image, then, of the interior metaphysics of photography: where only the past is privileged, where memory is reduced to the minimalist sign-form of an indigo-like blackness, and where the exterminism of feeling, a fatal melancholy, is the felt aesthetic. These are not paintings of a culture outside of ourselves, but interior snapshots of the post-catastrophe personalities of dissolved egoism. Alleyn's painterly imagination begins where the media finally come inside the body under the sign of the virtualization of the senses, and results in unrelentingly bleak tableaux of bodies without feelings, perspective, or subjectivity.

Bodies without subjectivity are created for vacationing in Nietzsche's noon-time sun, when the horizon is bleached free of meaning and eyes are only illusions of the presence of perspective. Everything is reversed. What we see on the outside (*Threshold, Amnesic's Playground, Amnesia Zone, Afterimage, Viewfinder*) is what is happening to *us* on the inside. What we see on the inside is a world of inertness and melancholy to such a degree of manic frenzy that it finally collapses, as does the line in *Hourglass* into time which stops, an endless waiting with no expectation of relief.

Or, perhaps something else. Perhaps Alleyn has painted the first metaphysical album of the will to photography with all its mutilated sentiments arrayed: melancholoy, anxiety, inertness, and vacancy. A perfect Nietzschian will to photography as the measure of the impossibility of viewing anything in the amnesic's playground. An "afterimage" of the optical self, where subjectivity is dissolved into the infra-red of a photographic negative. A world of technological possibility, but human impossibility, where the skin is like water, perfectly translucent and permeable: a medium without a meaning.

Is the photograph the aesthetic antithesis of human vision? If by vision we mean a vision of the world inscribed by memory, historical context, and inscribed emotions, then photography is the opposite. It is the privileged form of sight for severed eyes. At once an amplification of optics into a focussed view, it demands an immediate shutdown of memory. Photography, therefore, as the favored form of sight for the society of severed eyes, always at time's end, always decontextualized, always imploding vision into a fatal waiting zone of perfect inertness. So then, snapshot subjectivity for a culture marked by forgetfulness, yet bound by a fatal nostalgia for the seduction of the image.

Or is it the reverse? Photography as not the exteriorization of vision for a culture of severed eyes, but a fantastic acceleration of vision for acquiring a better sight-line for negotiating virtual reality. In this case, photography would be improved vision for the telematic body: an

Edmund Alleyn
Amnesia Zone, 1989

Edmund Alleyn
Afterimage

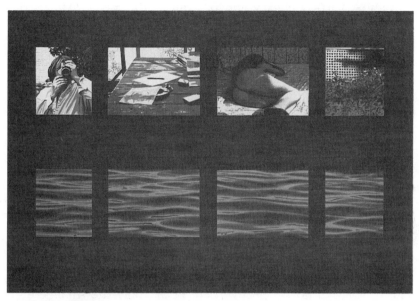

Edmund Alleyn
Reflections, 1983

Edmund Alleyn
Amnesiac's Playground

anamorphic space of doubled vision for seducing the perverted image of virtual reality. Photography provides an illusional space that speaks in the language of the ambivalent optic, a third eye for travels in virtuality. The will to photography is where facticity and staged communications flip back and forth as mirrored signs of each other's disappearance.

What is the perspectival space of the culture of severed eyes? Alleyn's answer is clear: the implosion of space into the disappearing logic of the sign. It is a semiurgical space where sight burns down to the optical horizon of indigo blue, and where no mediation exists between foreground and background. Here, only random alternations of drifting objects (*Relativity*) occur, a "twilight zone" intimating that we are on a "voyage to extinction." A post-catastrophic culture, where human beings have undergone such a radical severance of remembrance and sight that we are left with bodies that flip between hermeticism and schizophrenia. Thus, the special significance of a painting such as *Reflections*, where skin and water mutate into a surface-effect of languid emotions. There is no perspective here at all, only the shimmering reflection of surface events. A mirror of (faded) seduction that in nature (the water) and social nature (the sleeping woman, the photographer) exists under the fatal sign of the law of imminent reversibility. Except, unlike traditional romanticism, in the photographic tableau the mirror of seduction shatters to reveal the presence within of an interior darkness, an indigo subject.

CHAPTER SEVEN

The Virtual History File

Transiting to Nowhere

Two artificial games from recombinant America: one from the eastern
(software) seaboard of the U.S.A., and the other from the West (hardware) coast, and both on the 4th of July.

Playing in the MUD

MIT's newest artificial game—MUD (multiple user dungeon)—is a
perfect virtual reality simulator. Upload your electronic body via Internet
into the MUD, and you are suddenly exited into a strange, spectral,
disembodied space. In this floating fiction-packet you choose your own
"handle" and take verbal hits emerging from unexpected points in the
virtual geometry from other nomadic travellers on the electronic frontier
(voices come at you from up, down, behind, sideways, and even from
inside your skin as the schizoid electronic self clammers to get out and
play in the MUD). The discussion in the MUD playground is banal, high
school existentialism: "What's the meaning of cyberspace?" "Is this all
there is?" "What are we going to do now that we are here?" But the verbal
screen is just that: a trompe-l'oeil that disguises the shocking intensity of
the feeling of dislocation from the flesh as your electronic mind floats
around in cyberspace. The sensation is like treading aerial water in a dark,
nowhere space where digital bodies converge momentarily like irides-
cent bubbles, and then just as suddenly burst and disappear.

Then you get it. MUD is not really an artificial game in the VR
construct line, but the operationalization in ludic terms (in the sim/
sandboxes of the virtual class) of a new theory of the origins of the
universe: bubble physics. An article in the science section of the *New*

York Times breathlessly reported on the newest (techno)cosmology: the universe did not begin with the "Big Bang" after all, but with the bursting of the bubble. In this theoretical rave-scene, it all begins with the bubble, in fact with zillions of bubbles taking the mutating form of ocean foam. Consider John Noble Wilford's description in the *New York Times* of July 6, 1993:

> Hardly anything matches the evanescence of bubbles, those fragile watery spheres filled with air that have but a moment before they dissolve or burst. Time enough, though, to enchant with their iridescence in sunlight, give scented caresses in a warm bath, or tickle the nose over a champagne glass. Even time, perhaps, to have set in motion chemical reactions that led to the origin of life. The role of bubbles in the creation of life on earth is one of the newest approaches to solving the scientific mystery that is probably second in importance only to the problem of how the universe itself began.
>
> No one is suggesting that bubbles might explain everything. But in a new hypothesis receiving close attention, the multitudes of bubbles forming on the surface of primordial seas must have collected chemicals and concentrated them for synthesis into complex molecules. Eventually, through multistage reactions constantly repeated by uncounted generations of bubbles, the molecules grew in size and ambition, ready for the transition to living, reproducing cells.

That account fits MUD: an electronic bubble, without depth or permanence, floating, simultaneous, and immediate, washing up on the shore of the virtual beach like phosphorescent (VR) foam, and then disappearing back into the data sea. MUD, then, as the evolutionary beginning of the primordial sea of life in the electronic void, a (data) ocean/(human) atmosphere interface for the prebiotic origins of the molecular development of virtualized flesh: cybernetic foam.

Playing in the MUD is the pataphysics of New Age culture. It is how the western (technocratic) mind likes to think of itself in the dying days of the twentieth century: evanescent foam in the evolutionary story of virtualized life. Not so much, then, a new (bubbles) physics, but the aesthetics of the technocratic mind uploaded into a theory of physical cosmology, only to better serve as a recursive image of the beautiful virtualized mind: frothing away like the "evanescence of bubbles, those fragile watery spheres filled with air that have but a moment before they dissolve or burst." Consequently, playing in the MUD consists of a (virtual) childhood regression where the "bubbles matrix" becomes the new physics and bubble physics itself becomes the key literary fiction of the New Age.

Speeding to Nowhere

A fellow traveller on the virtual road appears on the cyber-net scoping out the San Francisco techno-scene. It seems that the big event on the 4th of July was a virtual reality cookout at the cyber-corral: a huge techno-rave with thousands of participants, most of whom lined up to try on a virtual reality helmet at twenty-five dollars a pop. Skin your head into the VR helmet and you are flipped instantly into electronic sim/ space with another parallel rave in Los Angeles, where Timothy Leary is the exuberant host. In this version of cyberspace, you reenact the violent sacrificial rites of the founding of America as the world's leading exterminist culture: ravers in San Francisco and L.A. engage in virtual shootouts in virtual badlands, hunting down and vaporizing electronic images of other players by means of the pixel-flashes of the heads-up visors and with fibre-optic automatic weaponry.

Is such war play a perfect fusion of technological fetishism and the primitive ecstasy of the culture of violence? Or something else? The word on the techno-streets of San Francisco is all about AT&T's newest promotional slogan: "*Be There Here.*" A cute twist on the virtual logic of simultaneity and immediacy as the always existent property of old electronic technologies of communication, telephones most of all. Here the telephone is imported into the sim/scan of virtual anamorphosis and presented for what it is: a work of high digital art that disappears space into a pulse of mirrored, recursive space: "You only know you're (virtually) there, because you're (actually) here." Just like the techno-ravers in L.A. and San Francisco, whose bodies are walking promo bursts for the inauguration of the new American virtual time-zone of there/here space, where you only know you are (actually) here because you are (virtually) there.

Virtual reality sells the illusion of displacement. It allows you to jump out of the inertial drag of skin and bones, and patch into the cybernetic side of your schizoid other, leaving the "there" behind like a burning car wreck that quickly recedes in the rear-view mirror as you zoom down the freeway on the way from nothing to nowhere.

Artificial games are the reality-principle of virtual culture: real cyber-netic flesh, real vaporized eyes, real data organs. A strange matrix of play-functions for travelling across the electronic frontier. Ludic only because they are work training sessions for virtualized flesh, artificial games have a veneer of imaginative fantasy, but an inner reality of reworking the organic body into its virtual replacement. In this mirrored universe, things appear only in their opposite sign-form: games are, in fact, hard cyber-work for virtualized flesh. Artificial, here, means the grubbly street materialism of a new (cyber) reality-principle, in which fantasy is the projection of the operational logic of telematic life onto the body electronic.

In virtual culture, the only interesting artificial game is life itself: that hybrid world of organic flesh that has been left behind as excess ballast when virtual reality launches into the stratosphere of cyberspace. Once in a while, virtual bodies that have lost their way in the maze of cybernetic dungeons, and strange attractors have been known to accidentally download into the body organic, finding themselves in an eerie world of air, trees, and bio-organs breathing without technical support-functions. Like amphibians struggling out of the primordial muck of ocean foam, virtualized flesh has to learn anew the artificial game of earthly life. But it never will. It is speeding to nowhere.

Recombinant History

The millennium is most certainly not the "end of history" so lamented by all the conservatives, nor a period of "post-history" as trumpeted by liberal historians, but, most definitely, the beginning of recombinant history. We live, that is, at the edge of a fantastic intensification of a history that is yet to be written: the telematic history of the virtual body. It is a history marked by a double moment: its reflex, the archiving of the horizon of human experience into relational data bases; and its dynamic will, the creative recombination of our telemetried past into monstrous hybrids that will form the incisions of the electronic landscape of the twenty-first century.

While the "end of history" thesis had use-value as an explanation for the fading role of ideology in the twilight days of the Cold War, and the perspective of "post-history" expressed insightfully the eclipse of the referential illusion of modernist history, recombinant history is the telematic future of virtualized flesh. Here, the (virtual) history file compresses the electronic body into a universal digital archive, always available for sampling, triggered by system operators at its XY axis, and indefinitely recombined into hybrid images of the telematic future.

No longer localized in bounded energy fields, virtual history is finally free to produce recombinant images of life once the organic body has been fitted with a customized nervous system. Expressing perfectly the ruling mentality of the virtual class, recombinant history archives the human condition in the form of its smallest elementary data particles, and then, as Data philosophizes in Star Trek, "reassembles the body as a machine." Pushed from behind by the will to (data) archivalism and pulled from ahead by the will to recombination, virtual history recounts how electronic flesh comes to full self-consciousness, how the digital body becomes aware of its abandonment of the drag-weight of skin as it synchs smoothly with its bio-machine interfaces. The virtual sex archive beckons to us from the welcoming shore of a third sex, a floating sexual screen where gender signs go to ground, as the electronic body flips into the non-space of the ecstasy of anamorphosis. The electronic body' archive scans the future of organs without a body, perfectly fibrillated and hyper-charged for nomadic journeys across the media-net. The military-entertainment archive seduces it with its telematic vision of a logistics of perception, so precise in its greenish thermal infra-imaging that data becomes the only battleground: the event-horizon of the war machine as the indispensable entertainment conglomerate for virtualized flesh.

In recombinant history, archiving is always on its way to recombination into a new configuration. Electronic bodies merge: the consumer body is a war machine; the medicalized body has its financial history stored in the spooling gateways of hospital computers, waiting to be leeched (recombined) of the weight of its earthly possessions; and the celebrity body is a dead star, which, like the luminous brilliance of a "red dwarf," is understandable only by the rules of deep space astronomy. Just when we thought that history as a *grand récit* had finally died as the last victim of the modernist illusion of misplaced virtuality, suddenly it returns in full recombinant force: that point where history merges with digital technology, becoming the world-historical process animating the will to virtuality.

The Electronic Abattoir

Sysops (system operators) have discovered that they are they are
monarchs in the electronic kingdom.

Colin Macdonald, *Internet e-mail*

Archivalism is power: The power to download the body into data, to
screen the body electronic, to file, delete and recombine the body in its
virtual form as a relational data base into new configurations. Archivalists
are Nietzsche's body and conscience vivisectionists, vampiring organic
flesh, and draining its fluids into cold streams of telemetry. The grey
unnoticed language of archivalism, with its process commands, dull
authoritarian style, and flat ascii personalities masks the transformation
of dead labour (recombinant commodity) and dead culture (recombinant
sign) into dead information (recombinant history). Violently detached
from the body organic and freed from local, bounded space, the matrix
of dead information floats away as bursts of "packet" sized data. No longer
information in the semiological sense, but the archived body parts are
disguised in the binary functionality of data and pooled into larger
circulatory flows. Medievalism might have been characterized by "bleeding" through the application of leeches to the skin as a medical practice,
but recombinant history gives us virtual bleeding: the harvesting of
energy from the local and the bounded for the global and the unbounded.
Archivalism is the politics of cynical history: virtual leeches on the
fibre-optic skin of the electronic body.

Rejecting the great referential language of juridical power, never
having known the commodity in anything other than its recombinant
form, neither reducible to a passive storage function nor to automatic
(data) reproduction, archivalism is something very different. It is a
bio-power: the creation of the virtual history of the electronic body by
detaching telematic information from its organic economy. Its aim: the
transformation of human experience into the dull codes of binary
functionality. Its destiny: the smooth merger of the (virtual) individual
file with aggregate data. Its emblematic sign: the speed and immediacy
of the data retrieval function. Its astronomy: a continuous circularity of
the (virtual) history file as the starlight of the electronic kingdom.

In the electronic abbatoir there is an intensification of the will to history: a molecular history of the body relating the health of its (failing) organs, its consumer preferences, the videos it has eaten, its screenal economy of telephone junkets, its political preferences, and its financial data. A minutely calibrated data scan of the detritus of the body collects material which are coldly archived as the electronic data-stream of the organic body flares through cyberspace and, like a dying comet, burns off its excess material in the form of electronic debris. A nano-history of the (filed) electronic body not only includes surveillance by the "monarchs of the electronic kingdom," but the archiving of the body's functions. Rupturing with (durational) time in favor of (virtualized) space, and refusing narrative closure on behalf of violently edged event-scenes, recombinant history expresses how the technological mind sees the world at the millennium: data is the real world, archivalism is the ruling reflex, logic is combinatorial, and the (virtual) history file is the last and best of all the fashion files.

Non-Time

> Science has certainly been pushed forward at an astonishing speed over the past decades: but just look at the men of learning, the exhausted hens. They are in truth not "harmonious" natures: they can only cackle more than ever because they lay eggs more often: though the eggs have got smaller and smaller. . .
> F. Nietzsche, *Untimely Meditations*

When history means the archiving of the human function and its recombination in the form of monstrous hybrids, then we can finally speak of non-history. The virtual history file as a transition to nowhere: a telematic process for growing history as a genetically engineered construct. This greenhouse for the clonal body is where culture plantings are snipped from samples around the electronic net, transcribed by the universal media archive, resequenced into new cultural hybrids, and cloned in the form of new body constructs. Because it inhabits dead time, virtual history has never been more vicariously alive.

Consequently, ours is a time of non-history that is super-charged by the spectacular flame-out of the detritus of the bounded energy of local histories. Two movements: the spreading out of the invisible (processed) history that archives the human function; and the explosion of local histories that, having no further use-value in the new superseded phase of ideology (the last stage of embodied history), flare out of control, like the swirling black clouds coming from those burning oil wells in the deserts during and after the Gulf War. A time of the always contemporaneous, non-history is a sampler machine rummaging through the media-net: a process of storage, retrieval, and recycling of all the detrital scenes of the movement from spasm to crash. Here, nothing is ever really lost, only downloaded into multi-layered relational data bases. Nothing is ever created, only instantly recombined by the resequencing of data strands from the past and future. And nothing is ever really experienced, only processed through the ether-net of virtualized flesh, like an invisible acid rain of neutrinos blasting through the earth's crust.

In non-time, local histories are fantasy worlds, maintained and periodically visited by representatives of the media-net for specular recombination into the entertainment function for the comfort zone tastes of the virtual class. Consider Somalia, a media theme park for testing the new colonial welfare model of the US/UN, but where something has gone spectacularly wrong. Somali mobs hunt down and kill western journalists, and US helicopter gunboats shoot last year's "victims" of the drought. Take the cynical piety first emoted for Bosnia, but quickly followed by media irritation with the Bosnian Muslims for not acquiescing in the liquidation of their country under the dictates of the Serbs and Croats. And even Yeltsin is fascinating to the media-net because he is an object of pathos: a walking theme park of ideology in ruins. Wherever he visits, Yeltsin curries favour by bringing a "gift" to the host state in the form of undisclosed secrets from the Soviet archive of the Communist Party. These gifts include: official state dossiers on American POW's for the U.S.A.; the flight recorder of the downed passenger jet 007 for the Koreans. What he does not understand is that no one cares any more about the secrets of the Soviet Communist Party. In the only archive that counts, the relational data base of the recombinant commodity-form in the empire of virtuality, the delete button has been pushed long ago on the USSR. Within days, it vanished from the media-net, simply disappeared from recombinant history, to be stored away for future telematic resequencing, probably as a TV serial. As the last of the true Communists, Yelstin is still trapped in the bounded space of the now vanished

Soviet empire, and it shows. Trading in the faded relics of the Cold War, Yeltsin's last use-value to the media is to prove that the Cold War actually existed, that the illusion of exterminism meant something, even if only nothingness. It's the very same in the West for the true recliners, the strategists of containment, who suffer most keenly nostalgia for the death of the referent of the Cold War. With the fall of the Berlin Wall, the delete button has been pressed on their memories. Archived for future recombination, their memories have been filed away in the data slipstreams of the ARPANET.

There are no longer any historical trends, only the disappearance of history into recombinant spectacles across the galaxy of the media. No longer the division of time into durational cycles of past, present and future, but into what Spengler has described as the premonitory shadow of "contemporaneity." In recombinant history, everything can be retrieved and rendered contemporaneous, so that the contemporary loses all meaning. History is resequenced as a fashion file. Virtual history consists of two primal movements: making everything available for digital archiving, and manipulating the archive into new, and ever more creative, recombinations. Consequently, the historical coda for the recline of the West: the retreat of the electronic population into fantasy worlds where bodies are prepped for virtualization by being saturated with recombinant images.

Telematic History

Telematic history is a virulent force. Driven by the will to archivalism, expressing itself by a spiralling combinatorial logic, policed by process administrators in their electronic kingdoms, and feeding on a mnemonic population, telematic history is the world-historical process of the age of virtual reality. Having no controlling referential signifier, telematic history trumps culture, supervenes over the expansionary and deflationary movements of the recombinant commodity-form, and is superior in the cybernetic chain of command to recombinant politics. Representing the merger of the world-historical process of the cynical sign and the will to virtuality, telematic history assumes the species-logic of a pulsating, virulent life-force. The most intensely abstract, yet most micro-materialistic, of the virtualized media of exchange, telematic history takes up its recombinant destiny on the stage of virtual reality with primal vigor. Here, through the global archiving of the human memory function it polices the passage of the body organic to virtualized flesh. Through the proliferation of hyper-technological fantasy worlds, by the surgical implantation of micro-chips into the skin, by the tattoing of retinas in the name of (virtual) pleasure, and by the IMAX(ing) of human and non-human history, telematic history enters into the blood-stream of the virtual body as its species-logic. Neither pure energy nor derivative code-element, neither value-principle nor coordinative stand-ard, telematic history sweeps onto the screen of the virtual body as its controlling element, just as the curtain is about to fall on the slaughter-house play of the twentieth century.

As the Leviathan of all the virtualized media of exchange, telematic history writes the text of the will to virtuality on the bodies of reclining flesh. It writes on organic bodies as they are dumped into the virtual window. It also writes on the bodies of corporations as pan-capitalism is resequenced into a servomechanism for the merger of technology and history. The will to virtuality is written as well on the electronic body of the media-net. Telematic history addresses itself to our always bored, but fascinated, attention in the displaced rhetorics of advertising, digitized music, and serialized imaging-systems. Relentlessly cyclical in its move-ment, telematic history repeats indefinitely the same rhythm of contrac-tion and expansion, but at progressively higher levels of abstraction and generality. In its contractionary phase, telematic history privileges the value-principle of archivalism: a reductionary sweep through the detritus of history in which the bio-human universe is reduced to the language of binary functionality. Typified by a maximum of process administration (of data) and by a minimum of creative recombination, the deflationary cycle of telematic history reaches its zenith in information gridlock. An immensely coagulated universe of slowly flowing data streams threaten to crash the system under the weight of a radical shortage of memory-function. If not abandoned to a state of terminal data meltdown, crash memory becomes the triggering mechanism that flips the switch on the expansionary cycle of telematic history. Here, archivalism is imme-diately sign-switched into its opposite: a floating recombination of the virtual history file into specious (futuristic) fantasy worlds. Marked by a maximum of new (integrated media) configurations, and by a minimum of data retrieval, the expansionary moment of telematic history involves a seduction to the sequestration-principle of its deflationary cycle. When the flat-line of data processing is finally eclipsed, telematic history is ready to indulge its pent-up appetite in the fantasies of cynical reason: not just the Luxor in Las Vegas, but the virtual world is landscaped by galaxies of media theme parks, and organic flesh is humiliated before the glittering fluidity of the virtual body. While the contractionary phase of telematic history is distinguished by technological fetishism (backed up by fear of unemployment or of being "out-sourced" by a competing national labor force), the inflationary cycle of telematic history is marked by recurrent bouts of technological euphoria. Anxious melancholy and manic buoyancy, therefore, are the psychological spectrum of recombinant history.

Beyond the class structure of the recombinant commodity (technological class versus working class), telematic history calls into being for its own advancement a further specialization of the class-function. A four-fold class structure divides the ruling virtual class into two programmer-functions: specialists (process administrators), who are responsible for supervising the war strategies associated with archivalism and recombination, and who assume, with a tremendous sense of hubris, full fiduciary responsibility for the maximum deployment of the (practical) will to technology. Then, cybernetically superior to the specialist-function, there exists a privileged world elite of historical leaders of the techno-conglomerates (from William Gates of Microsoft and John Sculley [formerly of Pepsi and Apple], who published his autobiography under the title, *An American Odyssey*, to Rupert Murdoch of the media world). Leaving behind the processed world of data engineers under the enterprising sign of "Details, details, I'm creative," the corporate directors of telematic history adopt a missionary sense of world technical destiny as their key value-principle. Finally liberated from (because wallowing in) the referential-signifiers of power, money, and social status, these cybernetic star-seekers are caught in an Olympian quest to represent in their bodily gestures and corporate strategies a creative merger of personal autobiography with the world-historical process of virtuality. This privileged corporate elite is the embodiment in the flesh of telematic history: pure virtualities, pure extensions of the will to virtuality, degree-zero points for the cancellation of all the (technological) signs. Whereas in another (medieval) age prophets were labelled witches of the devil's occult and promptly hunted down and killed by a resentful population, now they are sanctified as apostles of a new state of (virtual) grace. Nietzsche's gallery of cynical reason.

The programmed class of recombinant history divides into workers and the dispossessed, just as the programmer class of telematic history splits into its specialist and generalist functions. Localized in the bounded space of labor and tied, for its very existence, to a virtual exchange-relation based in time, the working class is a data archive to the recombinant logic of the specialist and directorate classes. Filed away in the laboring-archives of telematic history (factories, office towers, product assembly plants in the Far East, Mexico, and North America), the working class struggles everywhere to hold on to its own materiality of exchange-value at the very moment that the laboring body is fast-transited to virtualization. This is a cruel and fundamentally unequal struggle between the workers, whose very participation in the labor function of pan-capitalism condemns them to become standing-reserve for the virtualization of the exchange-relation, and the programmer class which, siding with the species-logic of telematic history, stands ready at every moment to liquidate once and for all the working-class because it is the rival of the emergent bourgeoisie, from industrial- and merchant- to pan-capitalist. Marked by the smashing of unions, the labor archive is corrupted from within and virtualized from without, as workers are driven back into the dark density of the sign of pure programmed-(labor) functions. And, of course, the "disappeared" of telematic history comprise the global class of the dispossessed: those with no program function in the unfolding of telematic history, and who are, thereby, deleted from the species-logic of the will to virtuality. While conglomerate directors are dominated psychologically by repression (they actually become their sign-function), and specialists are controlled by the category of social suppression (a limitation of their social [read professional, technological] possibilities), workers and the dispossessed suffer two very different modes of cybernetic domination. In the end-game of pan-capitalism, as it utilizes deficit management as a war strategy for inculcating fear and anxiety in the working class, workers are injected with crippling doses of political coercion ranging from the "work or starve" ethic of primitive capitalism to extortionary wage concessions and union-busting "agreements" between a radically weakened labor-force and the predatory class of corporate managers. The dispossessed are held in a permanent state of economic demobilization, corralled in holding-pens (from concentration camps for refugees to system-deleted countries) by the policing institutions of the international security state: the United Nations and the International Monetary Fund.

As (virtual) metaphor to (human) metonymy, telematic history benefits from each movement of its deflationary and expansionary cycles. In its archivalist phase, the positive motivators of "historical destiny" and "fiduciary responsibility," and the negative attractors of "intense economic fear" (for the working class) break down traditional barriers to the digitization of human and non-human experience. In the deflationary cycle, the humiliated flesh of the organic body comes to believe that virtuality is superior to life, that dead labor is better than living labor power, dead (recombinant) signs more meaningful than human culture, and recombinant memory preferable to material history. Humiliation before the perverted image and the ecstasy of anamorphic space are the hallmarks of history as cold telemetry. In its inflationary cycle, recombinant history is under the triumphal sign of a transition to virtualization. With a euphoric universe of integrated media, refinements in virtual reality generators and fabulous fantasy worlds (where the seduction principle meets techno/eco fascism), this phase of telematic history is fully co-extensive with the will to virtuality. Here, technology is freedom, because the recombination of living body parts into virtualized flesh promises the possibility of the endocolonization of death. Death is virtual because life is telemetry.

If archivalism and recombination are the value-antinomies of virtualized (historical) exchange, this would translate politically into revanchist (archival) political movements that seek to warehouse life in monumentalized networks of dead data. The illusion of the "national debt" and its use as a political strategy in the deficit management of the disciplinary state (its slogan: "zero-debt in four years") is archival politics. Like an arc that stretches across the electronic horizon of the virtual world, archivalism is the gold-standard of retro-fascism: Perot, straight from the networks of electronic data management, wants to fulfill Nietzsche's prophecies (in inverted form) by "letting the dead (debt) bury the living." Le Pen's *National Front* in France, Berlusconi's *Forza Italia*, and Zhirinovsky's *Liberal Democratic Party of Russia* share the archivalist tendency in cybernetic history. The rallying political obsession focusses on the retrieval of a previously warehoused possibility: an

"Aryan" France, a pre-Renaissance Italy, an insurgent, revolutionary Communist Party in the broken network of the USSR.

Arrayed perfectly against archival politics, although negatively and symmetrical with its reductionism, stands the historically expansionary domain of combinatorial politics. This is cybernetic liberalism: the new social contract for the networked body proposed by the Clinton hologram. It is also evidenced by Mitterand's creation of a recombinant state architecture (the telemetried Paris Opera House that stands opposite the fading sign of the Bastille, the new French National Library with its vaporization of books into information processes, the spreading of the speed-network of the TGV). Cybernetic liberalism is combinatorial: it breaks away from the retrieval function in order to create a new telematic matrix. The "digital superhighway of high-speed data" is neo-medievalism for the New Age. Our choice: the archived ego in the "selfish me" of New Age neo-romanticism, or the recombined ego of liberal fascism, where the ego dissolves into a pure extension of telemetry. Cold data warehouses of the (electronic) mind with a romantic veneer of kitsch medievalism (crystals, chants, and wilderness drumming for the hysterical male), or the virtual mind as a mini-theme park, filled with spurious desires, strolling voyeurs, and liquid TV flesh.

Crash Theory

Teilhard de Chardin's "noosphere." Marshall McLuhan's "global village." The notion of an emergent form of being that comes out of the "human" and surpasses it. Samuel Alexander's "deity" and all the other "gods" that humans are supposed to bring into being and which were in the minds of James, Bergson, Unamuno, and Whitehead. For the most part evolutionary and progressive. Also Hegelian. Just because the human will be decentered and surpassed by a new mode of being does not mean that the human will be diminished. On the contrary it will come into its own as collaborator in something greater. Honored collaborator. James's god was a friend and a partner who needed us. Whitehead's god was fulfilled only in its consequent nature through our efforts.

McLuhan's technological humanism stands at the end of this modernist discourse. All the other emergentists were visionary anticipators with theological imaginations. In McLuhan the noosphere materializes as the media-net. The emergent is no longer to be striven for as something in the future, but a fact. McLuhan is the moment of *positivistic* emergentism. He is reporting the *fact* that there is a mode of being that has succeeded and now encompasses the human. But he is still a humanist. He is still a doctor. He needs to prescribe. For him, there is a common sense which might be trained to respond to the distortions created by technology and to restore its homeostasis through an intelligent media diet. The media might yet serve "man."

Cross McLuhan's nervous system outerized by the media, with Nietzsche's "last man" (the first unequivocal sighting of the recliner) and you get crash theory. This is how it happens: Crash theory is the post-humanist (not anti-humanist—what is there to be against if the "human" is dead and now a subject of endless resurrection effects?) continuation of emergentism. It follows McLuhan's outerization thesis, and extends and elaborates it by calling attention to how the media-net is constituted by technologies that were not in McLuhan's ken. Crash theory, however, abandons the notion that media are "extensions of man." Far from it. They are humiliations of the flesh, which remains as an embarrassment after "man" dies.

The crash has happened. The emergence of the media-net is accompanied by the onset of reclining life. Rather than McLuhan's Hegelian vision of a common sense *restored* by and through the media, a media-net scans, sucks and probes the body for more images and bytes to be archived, called up, recombined, run, and archived in cyclical processes leading nowhere: that is non-history.

History is an irrelevancy because its subject "man" is no longer the protagonist of anything but cynical dramas on the media-net, and dead ideologies. There is no protagonist, but there is a mode of being emergent from the flesh that displaces all protagonists. Telematic being has no history because its only principle is the endless exchange of data, combined in every possibile form. Any of the directions that it seems to take are determined by the vicissitudes of the reclining flesh, which provides it with a (rotting) biological infrastructure (a resource base and an incitement for resource organization).

Telematic being, indeed, can never free itself from some form of the flesh any more than the flesh can free itself from the mineral kingdom. Androids synthesized especially for the process of providing images (data) and registering them consciously (bringing them into "appearance") are the ultimate answer to the media-net's requirement for a biological infrastructure. It hardly need be mentioned that these "androids" would not require any structural resemblance to the human body. As we are told ad nauseum by technotopians, silicon dryware will probably be far more effective in producing consciousness than the wetware that *homo sapiens* has become.

That is all in the "future," however. Right now the media- net would cease to be without activation through the flesh.

The flesh has crashed and is in a transition (virtualization) into the media-net to nowhere (to "cyber-space"). There might, however, still be "histories" of the vicissitudes of the flesh in relation to the media-net: history within an emergent historyless mode of being in which everything is contemporaneous and drawn from archives into recombinant narratives. This would not be the history of heroic struggles, whether micro-resistances or global revolutions, of flesh against the media-net; but would be chronicles of the abuse (value) of the flesh, reports on virtualization and the ways in which the flesh was react(ivat)ing to it.

The complications of the flesh and the media-net (telematic being), all the variations in the field between the complete replacement of the flesh by techno resource-receptors and retro-fascist primitivism, are the subjects of these studies and probes. From the viewpoint of modern history the moment of recline would be the next period after progressivism. But could modern history fit recline into its episteme? For non-history, recline is not a historical period at all but a symptom of the emergence of telematic being as a distinctive and pre-emptive (and peremptory) mode of being. Perhaps it would not be accurate to say that there might still be "histories."

The flesh has crashed and is in recline. (Retro-)fascist spasms should be viewed as nothing but instances of rebellion within recline, even though there is, if Peirce is right in general, some probability coefficient attached to the possibility that the flesh will short-circuit its (interminable) slow death with quick annihilation. Within the horizon of recline there are two possibilities—the literal abbatoir and the virtual (also in the "long" run literal) abbatoir. Quick or slow death of the flesh.

In recline the flesh takes itself with terrible cynical seriousness. Histories of every possible group and individual are collected and archived. Measures are adopted to save the flesh of the virtual classes.

The body, therefore, becomes a subject of innumerable "rights" for the virtual classes. But all this is an obsession with that which has already been superseded and is present only as infrastructure and abuse value: the body is thoroughly cynical and exists to disguise the disappearance of the flesh. To recapitulate: some visionaries at the beginning of the twentieth century announced (prophesied) the emergence of a mode of being out of "man." McLuhan, the last prophet, declared the advent of the emergent. Crash theory shows the consequences of the emergent.

In itself the media-net is universal. First, it does not distinguish among images by worth. It does not exclude. A gay in a military uniform is as good as a straight. Both images can be uploaded from bodies and downloaded into them. Second, the media-net is omnipresent and telematic. Upload a skinhead in Leipzig and download him in L.A. Everything is exchangeable. Thirdly, the media-net is recombinant, allowing all possibilities of connection to and disconnection from images and sound-bytes.

Telematic being circulates and mutates in a cycle in which bodies are uploaded into and downloaded from the media-net, producing a dizzying succession of hybrid monsters.

So Much for Paradise

The class struggles of the virtualization process occur within the horizon of recline. One great tendency is the formation of a virtual class, comprised of directors and specialists, with its internal tensions. The mission of this class is to deliver the flesh to virtuality, to telematic being. A second great tendency that counterpoints the first is the rebellion of the flesh against virtualization in the form of retro-fascism. This rebellion consists of a brutal quest for purity within the (vanished) flesh—flesh congealed into a fictitious societal community, a regression from virtuality to ideology! Lenin is in ruins and so is Reagan (Thatcher): retro-fascism is the only game in town for the bunker mentality, for the flesh that is under such terrible pressure as technology is oriented to virtuality within a pan-capitalist structure of hyper-exchange and hyper-speed. That which is resistant to exchangeability perishes in pan-capitalism, for it is the servant of virtualization.

Pan-capitalism mediates the complex relation between virtual class and place-bound classes from the perspective and goals of the virtual class. The state bureaucracies mediate that relation from the side of the place-bound classes—they should be called provincials and their opposite numbers virtuals.

The relation between virtuals and provincials is complex because each side contains something of the other. In the last analysis, the place-bound classes are destined to virtualization by their own reclining will. A couple of years ago a reporter interviewed a demonstrator at an anti-American rally in Teheran who declared that his fondest wish in life was to visit Disneyland. So much for paradise. Remember the road from Kuwait City into Iraq during the Gulf War, clogged with every imaginable vehicle bearing every imaginable consumer good? Remember how it looked when that consumer convoy got Bushwacked and ended up as a humongous junk sculpture exhibit exceeding the wildest fantasies of any environmental artist? What with the oil fires exploding and the fireworks over Baghdad each night this has to count as one of the greatest performance pieces ever mounted—courtesy of the military-entertainment complex with the special cooperation of Saddam.

Retro-fascism is a losing proposition. The place-bound carry virtualization within their will, which is why *post-liberal* fascism (there is no post *liberal-fascism*) is cynical in the last analysis. Yes. We'll do it all over again. Just watch. The Holocaust, for example, didn't take place. Okay. Non-history. On the other hand, the virtual classes are still composed of (disappearing) bodies. The psycho-flesh of these classes has an extreme preoccupation with itself, its components falling into everything from medicalizing themselves in technological environments to New Age regimens. This is also a sign of panic flesh, just like the place-bound flesh.

The root class struggle is complicated by the internal struggle within the reclining flesh between crash and spasm. Pan-capitalist elites mediate the struggles by seducing the flesh into virtualization and exploiting it for virtualization. The state bureaucracies mediate those struggles by trying to localize the economy and circumscribe the societal community. Each mediator penetrates the other, making all the struggles tentative and interminable. All of it amounts to an elaborate set of ruses by which the flesh beguiles itself into its own disappearance.

Historical Excursus: Recombinant Information

The Information Club

I recently had a dream about the information club. Probably because I had just finished reading Bruce Sterling's account of post-(Communist) life and the Red Mafia, the dream begins in a crowded stairwell leading into "The Information Club" in a Moscow building. A woman is on the stairs dressed in a bright green dress. She is carefully inspecting everybody's passport looking, as she keeps saying, for "irregularities." When I enter the main room, it, too, is jammed tight with uniformed passport inspectors, preoccupied with the task of inspecting passports again and again.

The dream sequences to another cinematic shot. This time the woman in green is addressing a TV camera, carefully announcing that no one should be alarmed, all passports have been inspected, and that everything is in order. When I look around the room now emptied of passport inspectors, there are only broken toys on the floor, a crying baby, and the woman in green, who, having finished with the television broadcast, turns in her chair and begins to laugh hysterically. The Information Club runs on empty.

The End of Information

How should information be priced in the information age? That is the central riddle of the digital revolution.

Teresa Riordan, *New York Times*
April 6, 1994

Information is the digital money of virtual society: soft value for a soft (virtual) society.

A cybernetic medium of exchange with its own history of speed and slownesses, information circulates through virtual culture like data without a destination. Always liquid and circulatory, adding surplus-value only when exchanged, information is a recombinant life-form: the victory of the pure sign (of data) over history. This is the age of the information bank. Information is how we are *valorized*, actually monetarized, by the virtual class. Like monetarist theory with its visions of economic control by the violent application of state regulations to the social body alternatively constricting and relaxing the credit mechanism, the information bank can be cybernetically steered in deflationary and inflationary directions.

Data deflation? That's the state of information depression where data is driven towards its referential extreme. Approaching the planetary referent of meaning, information falls out of its high-trajectory orbit and comes under the fiery gravitational pull of history. At this point, the information bank undergoes a depression-like crash, with a classic run on the always (potentially) bankrupt information bank by the waiting crowd of data creditors. At the degree-zero of the transparency of meaning, information loses its degrees of freedom, is stripped of its cybernetic means of circulation, suicides itself by falling into pure use-value, and flops back into the referent of meaning that it thought it had escaped forever. In the state of information depression, the (value) of meaning overwhelms the (sign) of data, and information is not allowed to circulate freely as a cybernetic medium of exchange. Think of authoritarian politics (contemporary China or the USSR before the fall of the Information Wall). In these cases, the political control of information exchange cancels out data as a freely circulating medium of exchange. As a result, information is politically forced towards the gold-standard of a state-administered meaning system. Information depression is a state of oxygen starvation for digital culture: a narrow bandwidth for an anti-virtual society with pure history, but no (digital) signal.

Data inflation? That's the triumph of communication over information depression. Not data under the political sign of use-value, but a world oversaturated by information to such excess that it becomes pure signal. A state of "pure virtualities," information inflation is typified by the transformation of all the referents into freely circulating cybernetic media of exchange. Here, the gold-standard of (referential) meaning is abandoned forever, and data approaches the maximal exchange represented by the over-authorization of the pure sign of information, and the under-authorization of the coordinative standard of meaning. In periods of information inflation, pattern-maintenance is continually destabilized. A world oversaturated by data finally breaks beyond a consumer model of information (with its market-steered models [of scarcity] of supply and purchasing power), and instead falls under the sign of excremental data: information, that is, as a site of imminent cancellation, exterminism, and liquidation. While the state of information depression is characterized by a scarcity of information, but a surplus of politically controlled meaning, periods of information inflation are typified by a hyper-scarcity of encryption keys (meaning), but a hyper-saturation of pure data. Communication is the antithesis of meaning, as much as pure data reverses pure history.

As a recombinant life-form, information must steer between the Scylla of data depression and the Charybdis of data inflation. The cybernetic steering mechanism is controlled by four software control processes that function as the key war strategies of the virtual class: an information economy driven forward by digital conversion, an information politics focussing on global strategic alliances, an information society typified by soft surgery on the body recombinant, and a virtual culture that is multimedia, multi-platform, and multi-sensorial.

The Four (Soft) Functions of the Virtual Class

> . . . the youth of today are incredibly sophisticated media consumers. They have grown up on MTV, Nintendo, Sega—they move very fast and can have a satisfying experience in just a few minutes.
> Douglas Trumbull, creator of *Secrets of the Luxor Pyramids*,
> (AXCESS)

Soft Money: The Information Economy

A predatory war machine, the information economy infiltrates every aspect of society in order to secure (our) transformation from human flesh to virtualization. Serving the broader function of enhancing (our) adaptation to virtualization, the information economy is where material experience is reconfigured, as the new mass society of data flows. Driven by the ideology of facilitation, but in actuality a process of digitalization, the information economy is a harvesting machine for virtualized exchange. Organized around the recombinant commodity-form, information always seeks to escape the old world of capitalism with its demands for balancing use- and exchange-value, and to attain a chaotic economy of differential value. Technotopian in inspiration and only capitalistic by necessity, the information economy is how the cybernetic grid maps itself onto the material world.

Soft Power: The Information Leviathan

Information politics focusses on the creation of global strategic alliances as a means of allocating newly emerging structures of digital value around the interests of the virtual class. Thus, for example, there is such intense commercial interest in the rapid development of global satellite communications for multi-media network processing (data, text, audio, and video), because these transactions are formally about capitalism, but substantively about laying down a neo-feudal structure of virtual power of awesome dimensions. Motorola's Iridium and the projected alliance of Microsoft and McCaw are the future hardware of the twenty-first century. They do not represent multi-media network "carriers," as much as they do communication media for controlling the form, and thus, the flow of post-millennial data. The future of virtual politics can be seen in these global strategic alliances among the virtual elite: hierarchical, based on the unequal appropriation of digital values, processed by the cybernetics of multi-media data processing, and typified by the uplinking and downloading into the electronic body of sensory stimulation.

Inherently anti-democratic in character, the Information Leviathan operates under the control of the virtual elite. Maintaining the necessary illusion that their global strategic alliances are about making money and not reinventing (virtual) colonialism, the virtual elite rush to put fundamental hardware decisions in place before societies have had an opportunity to recover from the shock of virtualization, or to slow down the speed of digitalization. The political interests of the virtual class are always advanced by the ideology of facilitation. As William Gates stated about Microsoft's alliance with McCaw to create a network of 840 satellites for downloading multi-media data on a global scale: "It will help us deliver education and health to rural areas." Knowing that public debate on issues concerned with technology and justice can only impede the imperial politics of global strategic alliances, the virtual elite seeks first and foremost to operate exclusively on a planetary scale (thus avoiding regulation by any single national public policy interest). When that is impossible, they present their political strategies as hardware decisions requiring only regulatory approval based on technical details. Like occult sorcerers operating in the night, the virtual class fears the light of democratic debate, and thus works to maintain the real secret of the information economy: that is, that its goals are always necessarily about power, and only derivately about economy.

The Cyber-Net: Soft Health / Soft Sex / Soft Intelligence

Information society functions to integrate the missing mass of the social into virtual reality by tattooing virtual (televisual) norms from without on the surfaces of the electronic body, and by performing soft surgery on the electronic space of the imaginary from within. What happens when the body is cut and pasted into the information bank? Information is the name given to the laws of virtual politics inscribed on the flesh. Never subtle, virtual power works to incarcerate the body in a grid of pure virtualities. The cyber-net is about the *rendering* of the recombinant body.

In the cyber-net, the great referents of human history come alive again in recombinant form. No longer is a referential discourse trapped in a founding genealogical logic with its proscriptions of universal truth-value, but the delirious rescusitation of recombinant referents for a society without truth or meaning takes its place. Here, the field of referential value is torn away from its vertical history in the body human, and transformed into a homeostatic process of the exchange of the body virtual across the cyber-net. Soft health, soft sex, and soft intelligence, therefore, as war strategies by which the body is encrypted in the field of virtual norms.

Soft health? No longer is health a property of individual bodies, but virtual health becomes the optimum medical condition of digitalized flesh. Infinitely programmable, fully politicized, and always mutatable in its definition, the state of soft health is a service delivered to the virtual body by the managed health care centres of the virtual class. Just as Michel Foucault warned in *The History of Sexuality,* we now live in the age of the "power of life over death." Speaking the language of soft therapeutics, the virtual class does not approach the human species in the coercive name of the "Father's No" but in the name of the (medical) ideology of facilitation. The virtual class facilitates the processing of the body through the bio-apparatus of soft health by affirming the will to (virtual) life.

Soft sex? That's the sexual congress of the electronic body. A televisual sex where the body downloads its desires into the orifices of the cyber-net: sometimes imagistically (pornography), sometimes aurally (telephone sex), and sometimes tactilely (the new machine dispenser sex of the 'feel-nets'). Like the recombinant history of virtual medicine before it, soft sex is a service delivered by the virtual class in the form of managed sex care. That is, the management of a certain level of sexual satisfaction for the virtual body as its orifices are processed by the information bank. And why not? Information has a sex: a floating machine sex for telemetried exchanges. Long ago McLuhan intimated that the human species fertilizes machines, makes them come alive, and in return for the gift of virtual life machines reciprocate by giving human sperm banks wealth and power beyond their dreams. The age of soft sex, however, is also the time of the softening, and sudden reversal, of McLuhan. This is a period when it is no longer necessary for the human species to provide the cyber-net with the gift of reproduction, because the machines have gone recombinant, acquired the gift of virtual life, and have returned to their human donors with the final act in this sacrificial tableau. The cyber-net in the form of process health, process sex, and process knowledge seeks to fertilize the previously uncyberneticized body, to make it come (virtually) alive, to know the sexual pleasure of immersing flesh in the screenal body of virtual reality. When the body rubs against the charged static field of the scanner net and feels the electrical rhythm of cyber-love, then it knows that it has finally come home to its own sacrificial disappearance. The cyber-net has a sex, and that sex is coded by information flows, circulates in the telematic form of liquid data, and caresses the flesh in 3-D optical scanning images of the body organic. Virtualization is always about sexual exchange: process sex for bodies dumped in the name of virtual love into the waiting orifices of the scanner machines.

Soft Intelligence: The mind does not exist. It was always a trompe-l'oeil hiding the disappearance of intelligence into a relational field called truth-value. This disappearance is the beginning of soft intelligence: no longer the mind as a mirror of a truth hidden outside of itself nor the mind as a dull representation of sensory experience, but the reappearance of the virtual mind in recombinant form. The virtual mind is the electronic world of soft intelligence: a co-relational world of circulating data and imaginary spectacles. Not intelligence as the sovereign property of bodily minds, but the virtual mind as the cybernetic intelligence of process world. A "mind archive" that vacuums individual intelligence of its history, and on behalf of which the hapless figure of the "thinking self" becomes a willing cerebral servomechanism. When soft intelligence becomes the sovereign epistemology of virtual culture, then *Windows* is not really an operating-system for personal computers but a perspectival revolution by which the cyber-net acquires digital programming control of the fleshly remainders of the virtual mind. It is *we* who are windowed by a systems operating language: rendered into a telemetry function of soft intelligence.

Soft Values: Information Culture

The appearance of the virtual class marks the end of capitalism, and the beginning of the age of pure technology. Here, predatory capitalism is dragged onto the stage of world-history for one last appearance as the productive apparatus necessary to set virtualization in motion, but once micro-charged the virtual class bears only an antagonistic relationship to capitalism. The chief beneficiary of the information economy, the virtual class operates under the illusion that it is in control of the virtualization of history in the direction of pure data. Itself a class thrown into history by the mutation of the recombinant commodity-form into its purest expression possible as the information bank, the virtual class is itself a transitory servomechanism of the age of recombinant information.

When it will have succeeded to put in place the four key strategies of virtualization (digital adaptation, virtual reallocation, data integration, and micro-culture), it too will be consumed by the will to virtuality. Needing no necessary class alliances, loyal to no social interest outside of digitalization, taking on the form of floating software bodies, and having only a telematic intelligence for navigating through artificial culture, recombinant information is simultaneously the historical justification for and the future liquidation of the virtual class. Required at first as an energizing force for uplinking information into a cybernetic medium of exchange, the virtual class is destined to be archived, and digitally recombined, in the information storage bank. When the virtual class is itself virtualized then pure information is finally free to crack its way out of the shell of pre-digital culture, adopting the species-form of cyber-culture. Not a world typified by the death of all the referents, cyber-culture is typified by their fantastic reawakening in recombinant form.

The real fascination of communication lies in the possibility of the *end* of communication, just as the seduction of information is to be found in its disappearance. Communication always wants to shed the heavy responsibility of having to maintain a gravitational field to stabilize the orbiting trajectory of information; and information desperately wants to go to ground in the referent of meaning. Information desires its own liquidation in the polar flare-outs of pure data or pure meaning; as does communication demand to be physically separated from the historical burden of the grand signifier of information. Condemned to be eternally entangled, the orbiting planets of communication and information approach and recede from one other. Never attaining the escape trajectories of pure data or pure meaning, the doubled poles of communication and information stabilize in the violent metastasis that is cyber-culture. A closed world, ritualistically inscribed, and almost autistic, cyber-culture is the non-time in which human history is harvested of its surplus-energy by the will to virtuality. In the beginning was the Word, but in the end there is only the data byte: the virtual history file.

Data Flesh

Personal consciousness will have nothing to do with the fate of the flesh in the Net. The world of the Net is Hegel's "objective spirit" de-totalized and in the form of circuity. The geeks understand this and that is why they are different from the representative types of the virtual class—the technotopian visionary and the cynical, predatory computer-capitalist that are most often combined in varying proportions in a hybrid monster. The geeks value "interaction" IN the Net for-itself. They would rather have cyber-sex. They find "immersion" to their great liking. They are deployed within the Net CREATIVELY. The geeks love the experience of being dumped and they lend the soft matter of their brains to the process of making that experience a romp in surf city, the "open Net" that John Battelle of *Wired*, an ascetic priest, cynically closes in the name of inevitable capitalist hegemony.

The geeks have over-identified with the Net and have become in consequence INCEPTS. That will be the fate of everyone anyway—the geeks have embraced that fate in a Nietzschian data-dance. What differentiates them from a "standing reserve" to be "challenged-forth" into the Net for image/info processing and image/info reception is that they mutate the Net. They mutate it with everything from the data-trash of e-mail messages that lack the presence of speech and the discipline of writing, to the most subversive data-games. Perhaps Battelle is correct in claiming that the geeks will be muscled out by Time Warner, et al., but that battle is not over yet. The body telematic is subject to viruses. It is yet to be determined how much wet (if only) brain(-like) matter is needed to keep the Net sparking. The geeks have ingenuity and Nietzschian affirmation on their side. The virtual class is plunged in cynical technotopia and cynical capitalism. Two visions: A. The body as image/info resource and image/info receptor under the cynical signs of possessive individualism and predatory capitalism. B. The body as INCEPT being deployed creatively in a web-making process of interaction through the Net.

Geek Criticism

The incept consists of the body oriented to the Net for (participation in) the Net. The body as resource/receptor is a passive incept. The active incept is the body mutant, proliferating the bulletin-board flow. Into that flow move the hyper-geeks, aware that they are over-identified and, therefore, at a reflexive distance from their over-identification. But not in a retreat back to humanism, back to vinyl. The hyper-geeks are critics IN the Net, not OF it. They affirm inception.

The Intelligence of Artifice

Beyond capitalism, the twenty-first century will witness the triumphant ascendancy of the virtual class as the dominant historical impulse of the next epoch. No longer the age of pan-capitalism, the virtual class will rescusitate capitalism after its death, dragging the corpse of the Victorian capitalist production-machine onto the world-stage for one last cameo appearance before technology, in the form of the will to virtuality, finally sheds its skin to become the pure sign-form that it always yearned to be. Cybernetics is the command language of the helmsman: the steering-mechanism inserted at the vanishing point of virtual culture.

A virtual millennium of pure tech, Year 2000 is driven by the cold seduction of digital dreams. Really a return in hyper-garb of the age of Christianity. A new religious era in which the salvation myth is embodied in technical willing, where conversion fervor swirls through the air once more, and where the spasm priests take the (virtual) form of missionaries in the age-old quest of quick dumping recalcitrant flesh in favor of the pleasures of the virtual entertainment complex. St. John the Baptist is on the Net, and this time he is wearing a Nintendo power glove and cyberware scanning eyes for announcing the coming of the newest California hyper-Messiah of the day. Pure Tech churns personal histories into cyber-dust, twisting and turning the always failed search for a stable personal identity on which to hang one's hopes. But unlike the early days of Christianity where martyrdom was the coinage of redeemed flesh, the virtual century witnesses a stripped-down eschatology. It is the sacrificial tale of victims as (their own) executioners. A recycled culture for the Remake century glitters before us like a neon mirage on the shimmering desert landscape. A virtual sign without virtue for a millennium that opens on the screens of cyber-culture as the triumph of artificial intelligence, but without the intelligence of artifice.

Data Trash Glossary

We are data trash. And it's good.

Data trash crawls out of the burned-out wreckage of the body splattered on the information superhighway, and begins the hard task of putting the pieces of the (electronic) body back together again. Not a machine, not nostalgia for vinyl, and most certainly not a happy digital camper, data trash is the critical (e-mail) mind of the twenty-first century. Data trash loves living at that violent edge where total human body scanning meets an inner mind that says no, and means it. When surf's up on the Net, data trash puts on its electronic body and goes for a spin on the cyber-grid.

Adobe Photoshop Optics: Digital eyes for quick travel across the recombinant field of digital reality. No longer the vanishing-point of perspective as in the Renaissance, virtual reality is an anamorphic space where events unfold in the form of the perverted image. Adobe Photoshop inscribes electronic eyes with scanner vision: layering, pasting, pastiching.

Bunker State: The prevalent contemporary form of fascism which attempts to exclude "aliens" from its midst both for the sake of economic protectionism and for an imaginary of social purity.

Crash Culture: Contemporary society as it undergoes a simultaneous fatal acceleration and terminal shutdown. No longer Spengler's *Decline of the West*, but the Recline of the West at the end of the twentieth-century. Culture is already a field of dead power. Crash occurs after the exhaustion of all the master signifiers. Post-modem society is post-Crash society, where everything always speeds up to a standstill.

Crash TV: Speed surfing across 500 channels of dead ether going from nowhere to nothing. Or maybe just the opposite: regeneration through violence of the flagging energies of the social by making of TV a scene of sacrificial violence (see America's biggest crashes—*Eye Witness Video*; America's biggest accidents—CBS *Nightly News* with Dan Rather and Connie Chung; America's biggest cyber-mouths—late-night talk shows; America's biggest serial murderers—*Death Video* now circulating on college campuses.)

Excremental Culture: The recycling culture of the nineties. Contemporary society as a waste-management system, stockpiles dead images and dead sounds, and threatens to suffocate us with its inertia. Here, the media-net is a vast plumbing machine for managing the discharge of image effluents, and for recycling all the waste products, TV subjects most of all, produced by excremental culture.

Fascism: The worldwide state-form prevalent in an era of managed depression and pan-capitalism. Its essence is the imposition of punitive disciplinization as the privileged agent of social control and sacrificial social purification.

Liberal Fascism: Disciplinary liberalism as the effective regime in so-called "industrial democracies." Disciplinization is used to create a hospice society in which the population is mobilized as image/information resources and image/information receptors. Liberal-fascist rhetoric stresses international economic competition as the ground for discipline (see Bunker State). It promises security through the technological invasion of life-space (see Media-Net). It is the (interminable) transition to virtualization.

Retro-Fascism: The return to classical fascism, which was not supposed to ever happen again. Disciplinization is cynically used to create sacrifices of flesh in rituals of purity (see The Will to Purity). When conditions of economic depression combine with a sense of national humiliation, (retro-) fascism arises.

Incept: The body oriented to the media-net (for participation) in the Net. The *passive incept* is an image/information receptor. The *active incept* is a subverter of the control of the media-net by the virtual class.

The Internet: The extended nervous system of the electronic body. Internet flesh is an electronic nomad that travels the slipstreams and gateways of the digital superhighway.

Media-Net: Skinny dipping by electronic flesh. The worldwide communication complex that generates an electronically fabricated environment of image and information—the fulfillment of Marshall McLuhan's notion of the outerization of the nervous system. Ideologically figured as a utility for possessive individuals (the "information superhighway"), the Net is where bodies are dumped as data trash.

Neural Chips: When flesh goes electronic, then the brain must be patched into the processed intelligence of cyber-culture.

Nostalgia for the Body: Human flesh has been left behind, abandoned by virtual reality. So it puts on the electronic garments of the Internet Body, and warp jumps beyond nostalgia for its own disappearance. Resequencing its retinas into organic screens for lasering movies directly into the mind, and warehousing the body in cyber-scanning machines, the human body plays the violent games of cyber-war in all the virtual entertainment centers. Intimidated by the glittering images of virtual reality, humiliated by its sluggishness compared to the speed of the media-net, and assaulted by the war machine of the virtual class, human flesh is a site of sacrificial violence.

Prozac: A psychic umbrella for a rainy day. Plastic surgery for the mind.

Pan-Capitalism: The economic situation in which contemporary capitalism for the first time is unchallenged, either by an artistocratic (traditionalist) or proletarian (revolutionary) opposition. Capitalism now has no critic and no organized opposition: it must try to take care of itself. Capitalist organizations rely on the ideology of disciplinary liberalism as a way of controlling labor, and appeal to fascism when they are in trouble.

Quick-Time Heartbeat: Software for programming the heartbeat of the electronic body. Always a schizoid, the digital body lives out two mutually contradictory extremes: total inertia (when the power is turned off and digital flesh crashes into a junk-pile), and total ecstasy (when the energy is switched on, and virtual flesh is quick-time expressed into fast circulation through the arterial byways of the virtual world).

Recline: "Hugo Boss kind of guy wants to meet Guess? kind of girl." (Montreal Personals). In recline, contemporary society gives up to the intimidating power of Technology and Culture, and submits, with fitful rebellions, to the process of virtualization. Safety and the "petty conveniences" are the master values of reclining life—a reaction-formation against the underlying death-wish—the wish to be replaced by technology.

RISC (Society): Introduced by the big three of Mac, Motorola, and IBM as the new systems-programming language for the Power PC, RISC is the computer equivalent of the public policy language of the "risk society." This language is about negotiating among difficult choices without upsetting the status quo. A perfect system for virtualizers, for those, that is, who want "fuzzy friendliness" without speed.

Telematic: Characteristic of the technologies constituting the Net, such as computer networks, TV, fax machines, and telephonics, that have the power to collapse distance instantaneously through image and information processing. Improved orifices for the body recombinant.

TIFF Psychology: In computer graphics, TIFF files are compressed digital code for working in multi-media texts. When the electronic body comes alive, TIFF double-clicks out of the language of computer programs, becoming a dominant personality type on the electronic frontier. TIFF personalities always hold something in reserve: elegant up front, they have about them the seduction of something concealed in their programming stats. Or maybe something different: the way virtual personalities are patched from one Net to another, their complexity enfolded in the language of time-compression, just waiting for that magic moment to unfold on the screen of (electronic) life with their previously hidden attributes.

Spasm: The state of living with absolutely contradictory feelings all the time, and really loving it: fascinated yet bored/panicked yet calm/ecstatic yet terminal/apathetic yet fully committed. 1) Terminal shudders that suddenly appear from nowhere, convulse the media-net in frenzied attention and then disappear from view, never to be heard from again (John Bobbitt's missing penis, the L.A. earthquake, Nancy Kerrigan's knee); 2) the TV image of O.J.'s Bronco on that slow, surrealistic drive down the L.A. freeway, like an electronic *Days of the Locust*; 3) a sampler music CD by Steve Gibson to take with you on your journey across the electronic frontier.

Virtual Reality: Where flesh goes to die and the electronic body struggles to be born at the fin-de-millennium. Strap on a head-mounted scanner, wire your flesh with digital trodes, slap smell patches on your data suit and take an out-of-body flight across the outer galaxies of cyberspace.

Virtual Culture: The substitution of a technologically fabricated spatio-(temporal) perspective for the spatial-temporal perspective of "ordinary" waking perception. The perfection of virtual reality is to constitute an environment (totality) in which the virtualized body is completely immersed and with which the virtualized body can "inter-act." Full virtuality would constitute an environment that would be felt by the virtualized body to be complete, but would not be felt by the virtualized body to be an incident within a more genuine environment.

Virtual Elite: Electronic rulers of the information superhighway. Masters of the electronic kingdom, the virtual elite usually swarm in digital hives, from Silicon Valley and Chiba City to the European cyber-grid running from Munich to Grenoble.

Virtual Class: The social strata in contemporary pan-capitalism that have material and ideological interest in speeding-up and intensifying the process of virtualization and heightening the will to virtuality. The elite components of this class include technotopians who explicitly advance the cause of virtualization through offering a utopia of juvenile power (virtual reality flight simulators in all the entertainment complexes), and cynical capitalists who exploit virtuality for profit.

The Will to Purity: The politics of the nineties: sexual cleansing, ethnic cleansing, intellectual cleansing, racial cleansing, Internet cleansing. The politics of an entirely fictional search for a purity that never existed and never will.

Will to Virtuality: The prevalent drive of contemporary culture to seek to give itself up to virtual reality and become an incept in the media-net. The will to virtuality is grounded in the fascination with technology as a reaction-formation to the death-wish.

Notes: Chapter 1

1. John Seabrook, "E-mail from Bill," *The New Yorker*, LXIX, 45 (January 10, 1994): 54.

2. *Ibid.*, 49.

3. *Ibid.*, 49-50.

4. *Ibid.*

5. *Ibid.*, 52.

6. *Ibid.*, 54

Notes: Chapter 3

1. G.H.R. Parkinson, *Georg Lukács* (London: Routledge and Kegan Paul, 1977), p. 26.

2. Franco Moretti, "The Moment of Truth: The Geography of the Novel," *Contemporary Marxist Literary Criticism*, ed. Francis Mulhern (London: Longman, 1992), p. 121.

3. *Ibid.*, p. 124.

4. Walter Benjamin, "The Work of Art in the Age of Mechanical Reproduction," in *Illuminations* (New York: Schocken Books, 1969), p. 233.

5. *Ibid.*, p. 230.

6. *Ibid.*, p. 228.

7. The concept of anamorphosis in relation to the third sex was first theorised in Arthur and Marilouise Kroker, *The Last Sex: Feminism and Outlaw Bodies* (New York: St. Martin's Press, 1993), pp. 18-19. We are indebted to the reflections of Alberto Perez-Gomez and Louise Pelletier for our understanding of anamorphosis .

8. For a full description of the historical genealogy of anamorphosis and its cultural horizon in relationship to "accelerated" and "decelerated" perspective, see Jurgis Baltrusaistis, *Anamorphic Art*, trans. Walter Strachan, (New York: Harry N. Abrams, 1977); and J. Baltrusaistis's introduction, "Anamorphoses," in *Anamorfosen: Spec Met Perstectief* (Amsterdam: Rijk Museum, 1975-76)/ *Anamorphoses: jeu de perspective* (Paris: Musee des Arts Decoratifs, 1976).

9. *Ibid.*

Notes: Chapter 4

1. In addition to studying the political strategy of the Trilateral Commission and deciphering the (side)texts of the Canada/US "Free Trade" Agreement and NAFTA, there is also an excellent anonymously authored analysis of the International Business Roundtable circulating on the Canada-L BBS of the Internet, posted by Dale Wharton on June 8, 1993. While this text does not draw out the implications for the technological class of politicized "trade" agreements or situate the analysis in light of the recombinant commodity-form, it focusses critically on the fungibility of the international labor-market and the undermining of local state sovereignty by a resurgent American empire. Here, the politics of "free trade" are forced to the surface of the seemingly-transparent background of international economics.

2. *Ibid.*

3. David Cook, "Farewells to American Culture, Work and Competition," *Canadian Journal of Political and Social Theory*, 17 (1-2),1994. In this review article, Cook argues eloquently, and convincingly, that Lester Thurow (*Head to Head*), Robert B. Reich (*The Work of Nations*) and John Kenneth Galbraith (*The Culture of Contentment*) are the leading representatives of the recline of the American mind. While Reich focusses on the spatial recovery of the disappeared working class (at the behest of the "technological class') and Thurow talks about engineering the new "European beast," Galbraith closes his eyes to the brilliant sun of Crash America.

Notes: Chapter 6

1. Edmund Alleyn, *Indigo: Tableaux, Dessins 1983-1990*, curated and introduced by Leo Rosshandler (Montreal: La Galerie d'Art Lavalin/Maison de la Culture Cote-des-Neiges, 1990).

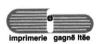
imprimerie gagné ltée

PRINTED IN CANADA